Life and Teaching of JESUS

Andrew Lawrence

illustrated by Richard Smith

MOWBRAY

To Sylvia my wife, whose loving patience made the book possible

Mowbray
A Cassell imprint
Villiers House, 41/47 Strand,
London WC2N 5JE,
England

First published 1990

British Library Cataloguing in Publication Data
Lawrence, Andrew
    Life and teaching of Jesus: GCSE assignment sheet
    photocopy masters.
    1. Jesus Christ
    I. Title
    232

ISBN 0-264-67191-0

My thanks to Robin Shepherd, Religious Education
adviser for Devon, for his Foreword.

Typeset by Colset Typesetters Ltd, UK
Printed and bound in Great Britain by
Hollen Street Press Limited, Slough

Contents

Foreword

Andrew Lawrence's work in the classroom is strongly influenced by his love of his subject and concern for the education of his students.

GCSE Religious Studies is a demanding subject which requires students and teachers to pay close attention to the criteria for assessment — that is, to understand what the examiner wants. Copies of these master assignment sheets will provide a clear working programme for studies of the gospel accounts of Jesus. It is very useful to have the key texts from the Bible readily available, so that time and other resources can be used for enrichment work around the main course.

If students negotiate contracts for learning and are involved in assessment the course will help to put into practice some of the objectives of the Technical and Vocational Education Initiative.

Robin Shepherd
County Adviser for RE, Devon

Introduction

These materials have been developed in accordance with the national criteria for the General Certificate of Secondary Education (GCSE), and can be used with most textbooks on the subject. They can also be used by those who are developing general studies for sixth-form pupils in this study area.

The original purpose of the task assignment sheets was to produce materials that are a positive response to TVEI (Technical and Vocational Education Initiative) and place emphasis on *learning* as opposed to teaching. The emphasis placed on organizing classrooms for learning has become greater, given the need to change practices for GCSE coursework studies.

Most schools now adopt 'resource-based learning' or 'supported self studies' as a method of working. Indeed, many schools have also begun to negotiate a contract with pupils, agreeing what the pupil will do and the time involved for an individual piece of work, or a whole module of study.

Naturally it is not an easy task to devise a time-budget, but as pupils of different abilities work at very different speeds, it may be helpful to negotiate with pupils what work each will do and the time factor involved.

The materials will give teachers the chance to create space for themselves when working with a group of pupils. This will be necessary for effective records of achievement and contextual tutoring. Formative assessment of social skills can only be made if a teacher can observe pupils while they are working together during lesson time!

Using the materials

It is not intended that individual study based on these materials should be the only method of teaching this course; teachers will want to use many other resources to vary the learning experience, and to cover areas that inevitably cannot be adequately covered here. But these assignment sheets can form the backbone of the course, or be used for extension study at home, for homework, for revision or for supply cover.

The materials take into account the varying abilities of the pupils. For specific, individual or small group teaching, the task sheet will enable the teacher to work with less able pupils on short, but quickly achievable goals, while the opinion and research sections, towards the end of the worksheets, should allow more able pupils to broaden the scope of their work. Each sheet starts with a simple activity designed to help pupils to record the basic facts of the story being studied, and works up to tasks with greater scope. The pictures are intended to help with the reading and understanding of the story; the parables are illustrated in modern dress to make the point that they were not historical events, but make points which are equally relevant today.

Although it has not been possible to avoid the occasional need to look at a dictionary, encyclopaedia, map or textbook, the Bible passages relevant to each worksheet are supplied at the back of the book, clearly numbered. Teachers may decide to duplicate and distribute all these pages for pupils to keep in their folder (so that there is no problem about not having a Bible at home and so being unable to do homework); alternatively, teachers may prefer to cut out the relevant passage for each sheet and duplicate it on the back of the sheet.

How the materials can be used will depend on the organizational methods adopted. Assignment sheets can be given individually to pupils, especially if they may find more than one task daunting. Assignment sheets can be grouped to form a module of work for those pupils who are able to consider a range of related tasks in a modular package.

The materials at the back

First of all, the most necessary **Bible passages** (from the Good News Bible) have been printed out, with pictures, at the back. Then **various sheets** have been included, which teachers will use or adapt as it suits their system, their division of the work into modules and establishment of the module aims, and the way they are integrating these materials with their course as a whole.

The teacher may wish to negotiate a contract with pupils, setting out clearly the expectations and commitment required of them. The outcome of such a contract will furnish some of the information needed for records of achievement (see the Module Contract, p. 85).

The sections on the miracles and parables readily lend themselves to a modular package. With imagination, selections can be made to form modules from the "Life and experiences" and "Positive and negative responses" sections, and also the Holy Week materials.

The grids for recording information at the back of this book may be helpful for pupils; they may require some experimentation.

When using the task sheets, you may ask pupils to copy the title, time allocation and assignment number on to a piece of paper, as this will enable pupils and teacher to keep a record of what has been covered. It is envisaged that the assignment task sheets will be handed back to the teacher on completion.

Many tasks ask pupils to "discuss and record". This may well be initiated by the pupils themselves in small groups working on the same task sheet. This method will serve to develop and share information as will the more formal, teacher-initiated 'whole group' discussions that will take place from time to time.

At the end of a single piece of work, or a module, it may be desirable for pupils to make a self-assessment of their performance. For this exercise, a self-assessment sheet has been devised, in simple language.

If pupils are going to make meaningful self-assessments based on criterion referencing, it will be necessary to have a wall sheet of the various levels of achievement and grade-related criteria. Pupils will need to refer to this wall display in order to make self-assessments that are criterion-referenced.

The levels of attainment grid at the back of this book is an attempt to set out basic levels of attainment and should be used carefully. It may not be relevant for the group you are working with and may need modifying. As with all criterion referencing, we are concerned with the attainment made by an individual. I hope the chart will be useful, or that you will be able to adapt it.

Two teacher assessment sheets are also included; they can be used to assess specific skills in the unit of work. In some cases, it may be that a single skill is assessed.

The cumulative effect of teacher and pupil assessments, made throughout the year, will contribute to forming a comprehensive record of achievement for each pupil in skills that are specific to the subject.

I hope the task sheets will be useful and that you and your pupils will enjoy using them. If you wish to contact me regarding the materials, I shall be pleased to hear from you.

Andrew Lawrence
Head of Religious Studies
The Park School
Barnstaple
North Devon

1: Matthew's account of the birth of Jesus

Objectives

To learn about the birth of Jesus from Matthew's Gospel.

To understand what the gifts represent in the story.

To find out if the birth of Jesus is an important event for Christians today, given that only two of the Gospel writers have recorded it.

I · THE LIFE AND EXPERIENCES OF JESUS

1 *Complete these sentences* after reading the story from Matthew's Gospel:
  (a) Joseph was anxious before he married Mary because . . . .
  (b) But in his dream the angel told him that . . . .
  (c) The baby was to be called Jesus because . . . .
  (d) Jesus was born in . . . . in . . . .
  (e) King Herod found out about his birth because . . . .
  (f) When Herod found out he decided . . . .
  (g) The three gifts the men gave Jesus were . . . .
  (h) The men did not go back to Herod because . . . .

2 *Find out:*
  (a) What does the word *conceived* mean?
  (b) What does *Immanuel* mean?
  (c) What word is now used to describe people who study the stars, like the men who visited Jesus?
  (d) Who was the prophet mentioned in the story?
  (e) From which direction had the visitors travelled?
  (f) What did each of the gifts symbolize?

3 *Opinion:*
  (a) Why do Christians believe that Jesus' birth was important? Read some Christmas carols and write down what explanations each give. Say in your *own words* which explanations make sense to you.
  (b) If Christians believe that Jesus is important, do you think that knowing how he was born is very important? Quite important? Or not very important? Read the opening passages of all four gospels: which ones tell about the birth of Jesus? Why do you think the others did not mention it? *Discuss* and then *write down* your ideas.
  (c) Has the real meaning of Christmas been forgotten? Consider this question and conduct an *opinion survey* in your group.

LIFE AND TEACHING OF JESUS   **I · The life and experiences of Jesus**

Assignment No.	
Time allowed	

2: Luke's account of the birth of Jesus

Objectives

To learn about the birth of Jesus from Luke's Gospel.

To compare Luke's account of Jesus' birth with Matthew's story.

To show how Luke is concerned to include outcasts in his Gospel stories.

1 Read Luke's account of the birth of Jesus and then *complete these sentences*:
  (a) When Jesus was born .... was the Roman Emperor.
  (b) Joseph went from the town of .... to the town of .... in .... the birthplace of King ....
  (c) Joseph was a descendant of ....
  (d) Joseph went to .... to .... with Mary who was promised in .... to him.
  (e) While they were in .... the time came for .... to have ....
  (f) Mary gave .... to her first .... wrapped strips of .... laid .... was no room .... inn.

2 *Find out*:
  (Use a dictionary for some questions, if necessary.)
  (a) What is a *census*?
  (b) Who ordered the census be taken?
  (c) What does the word *descendant* mean?
  (d) In which town was Jesus born?
  (e) What is a *manger*?
  (f) Where were the shepherds when the angel spoke to them?
  (g) What message was given to the shepherds?
  (h) Why is the town in which Jesus was born called "David's town"?
  (i) Which Christmas carol tells this story of Jesus' birth?
  (j) How might Roman records help to pinpoint the date that Jesus was born?
  (k) Try to find out the attitude of some people toward shepherds in the time of Jesus. Why was this the case?
  (l) Read again the story told by Matthew and compare it with the story told by Luke. Try to spot the differences, and *make a list* of them.

3 *Opinion*:
  Look at the differences in Luke's story: is it true that he includes less important people and outcasts in his story?

Text © Andrew Lawrence 1990. Illustration © Richard Smith 1990
Multiple copies of this sheet may be made by the purchasing institution only.

| Assignment No. |
| Time allowed |

3 : The Baptism of Jesus

Objectives

To learn about the baptism of Jesus.

To find out something of the character of John the Baptist.

To consider the importance of Jesus' baptism for Christians today.

1 Read the story from Matthew's Gospel carefully. *Match up the beginnings and endings of the sentences.*
Make a summary of this story: use a map and a dictionary if you need help.

Beginnings:

The Jordan is . . .

Baptism means . . .

John did not want to baptize Jesus because . . .

After the baptism, Jesus . . .

The dove was a symbol of . . .

The voice said . . .

Endings:

. . . the spirit of God.

. . . he felt that Jesus was better than him and should be baptizing him.

. . . a river in Israel.

. . . "This is my own dear son".

. . . came up out of the water.

. . . washing with water as a sign of the forgiveness of sin.

2 *Find out*:
How are people baptized today? Interview someone who has been to a baptism service and write your own account from the information given.

3 *Opinion*:
(a) What do you think people thought about Jesus when they saw what happened at his baptism?
(b) Do you think Jesus' baptism was important for his followers at the time? *Discuss.*
(c) Do you think the words spoken at Jesus' baptism are important for Christians today? Ask the opinions of Christians you know and record their views.
(d) Do you think baptism is important for present-day Christians? Ask the opinions of several people and record them.

4 *Research*:
Find out from a Bible and any textbooks available as much as you can about John the Baptist: where he lived, what he wore, who his parents were, who his cousin was, and how he died.

LIFE AND TEACHING OF JESUS

I · The life and experiences of Jesus

Assignment No.	
Time allowed	

4: The Temptation of Jesus

Objectives

To learn about the temptation stories and the differences in them.

To consider the importance of the temptations.

To show that Jesus spent time working out how he was going to conduct his mission and how he would approach the people with "the New Teaching".

1 *Find out*:
What are the meanings of these words from the two Gospel passages? (Use a dictionary if necessary.)
(a) desert, (b) temptation, (c) scripture, (d) worship, (e) angels, (f) Temple, (g) miracle.

2 Write a *short summary of the story*, saying where Jesus was, why you think he went there, how long for, and what ideas came to him.

3 Identify the differences in the two Gospel accounts: *make two columns*, one headed *Matthew* and the other headed *Luke*. In the columns make a note of any differences between the two stories. Say whether you think these differences are important.

4 *Make a list of ten things* that people nowadays might be tempted to do which are wrong.

5 Jesus was being tempted to spend his life in different ways from the way in which he was called. *Make three columns*, like the ones below, and fill in your opinions in the spaces:

Jesus was tempted:	If he had done this:	He did not do it because:
(a) To turn stone into bread.		
(b) To become the ruler of the whole world.		
(c) To show people he could do any miracle he wanted just to impress them.		

6 Study a newspaper carefully and *make a list* of the things that are going wrong in the world today. Do you think Jesus was right to decide not to become a dictator, or to put everything right by magic, but to challenge human beings to put things right themselves.

LIFE AND TEACHING OF JESUS   **I · The life and experiences of Jesus**

Assignment No.
Time allowed

5 : Jesus calls four fishermen to be followers

Objectives

To show how some people responded to Jesus and his teaching.

To appreciate further use of symbols.

To show that all "types" of people were ready to follow Jesus.

II · POSITIVE AND NEGATIVE RESPONSES TO JESUS

1 Read the story from Mark's Gospel carefully and *finish the sentences*:
  (a) Jesus went to . . . .
  (b) Jesus said, "The right time has come . . . .
  (c) Turn away from your . . . .
  (d) Jesus walked along the shore of . . . .
  (e) The fishermen were called . . . .
  (f) Jesus said to the two fishermen, ...
  (g) As soon as Jesus saw them . . . .

2 *Find out*:
  (a) What else happened in this story according to Luke's Gospel? (See Luke, chapter 5).
  (b) Look in textbooks and try to find out about the Greek word for "fish" and why it was used as a Christian symbol.
  (c) Why is Jesus' teaching called the "Good News"?

3 *Opinion*:
  (a) What do you think Jesus meant by the remarks he made to the fishermen as they were catching fish?
  (b) What slogan can you think of that sums up this story effectively?
  (c) Do you think the fishermen disciples were courageous or stupid when they left everything to follow a complete stranger? Ask others in the group for their opinions. *Write down* your views and the views of others.
  (d) How would you react toward Jesus if he returned to earth and asked you to follow him?

  Make a list of thoughts that you and others in your group might have.

Text © Andrew Lawrence 1990. Illustration © Richard Smith 1990
Multiple copies of this sheet may be made by the purchasing institution only.

Assignment No.

Time allowed

6: Jesus calls Levi

Objectives

To learn how some people responded to Jesus.

To show that there were often people who were against Jesus and his teaching.

To show that Jesus welcomed all people to change (repent) and follow him.

1 Read the story from Mark's Gospel carefully. *Make four columns*, like the ones below. *Fill in each column.*

Place(s) mentioned	People mentioned	Words spoken by all	What people are doing

2 *Find out*:
  (a) What does the word *disciple* mean? (Use a dictionary if you need to.)
  (b) Who joined Jesus as he ate with outcasts?
  (c) What other people would be regarded as outcasts other than those mentioned in this story?

3 *Opinion*:
  (a) Why do you think Jesus was hated by some people? Ask others for their views and *make a list* of possible reasons.
  (b) What lesson do you think others could learn from Jesus' words in this story?
  (c) Do you think it is harder to be a follower of Jesus today than it was when he was alive? Would you like to have been a companion of Jesus'?

4 *Research*:
  Find out what you can about the *costs* and *rewards* for anyone wanting to follow Jesus.

  Make a grid with the headings: *Costs* and *Rewards*.
  You may find the following references helpful: Luke 9.1–6; Luke 9.46–52; Luke 10.1–16; Luke 12.22–34; Luke 14.25–33.

  From these references *fill in your grid*.

  You may wish to work with others in a small group on this task.

LIFE AND TEACHING OF JESUS   II · **Positive and negative responses to Jesus**

| Assignment No. | |
| Time allowed | |

7 : Jesus heals a paralysed man

Objectives

To learn how the faith of some people influenced the way in which they acted and responded to Jesus and his teaching.

To be aware of the attitude of the teachers of the Law toward Jesus.

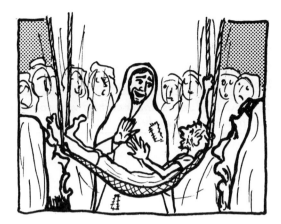

1 Tell the Gospel story *in your own words*, using the beginnings of each sentence to help you:
   (a) Four men arrived, bringing . . . .
   (b) It was impossible to get to Jesus because . . . .
   (c) So they . . . .
   (d) Jesus was able to help the man because of their . . . .
   (e) Some teachers of the Law thought the way Jesus spoke was . . . .
   (f) Jesus told the man to . . . .
   (g) The people around thought . . . .

2 *Find out*:
   (a) What does the word *blasphemy* mean?
   (b) What does the word *faith* mean? Describe in your own words.

   (Use a dictionary for these questions if you need further help.)

3 *Opinion*:
   (a) How do you think the man was cured?
   (b) Do you think healings like this still occur today? Give your views with examples.
   (c) Do you think there is ever a connection between feeling guilt and physical illness?

4 *Research*:
   (a) Some people, in the time of Jesus, believed that there was a reason why a person was sick, ill, or handicapped.
      Use a textbook; try to find out what people thought the reason was.
   (b) There are many incidents where Jesus was in conflict with the teachers of the Law.
      Use the Gospel stories and a textbook to find incidents that show Jesus being criticized.
      Write a *brief outline* of *three* situations.

8: The question about fasting

Objectives

To appreciate that some people were always looking for an opportunity to criticize Jesus.

To show that Jesus knew that he was soon to be taken from the people.

1 Read the story from Mark's Gospel and write the conversation Jesus had with the people who questioned him, *in the form of a play.*

2 *Find out*:
Use a dictionary and a textbook to answer the following:
(a) What is fasting?
(b) What does the word *Pharisee* mean?
(c) Use a textbook to find out who the Pharisees were and what they believed.
(d) Who is the "bridegroom" in this story?
(e) What are wineskins?
(f) What did Jesus mean when he said: "The bridegroom will be taken away from them and then they will fast".

3 *Understanding*:
(a) What evidence might suggest that Jesus knew he was going to die an early death? Support your answer by referring to the story.
(b) What was Jesus really saying when he spoke of "cloth" and "wineskins"? Discuss this and make a list of possible explanations. Look up this story in a textbook. What explanation is given?
(c) Who is the *bride* in this story?

4 *Research*:
Either
(a) Do people still fast today? Make a survey of 40 people of various age groups. Ask them if they have ever gone without food and what the reason(s) for doing so was/were.

Show your findings in the form of a *chart*.

Or
(b) Find out what different religions teach about fasting and *write a paragraph* about each.

LIFE AND TEACHING OF JESUS   **II · Positive and negative responses to Jesus**

Assignment No.
Time allowed

9: The question about the Sabbath

Objectives

To consider other negative attitudes toward Jesus.

To show that Jesus' attitude toward the Sabbath was different from that of the Jews who criticized him.

To learn about David (from the Old Testament).

1 Read the story from Mark and *correct the errors in the following translation carefully*:

Jesus was walking by the seashore on Thursday. As his disciples walked, he began to pick flowers. The teachers of the Law said to Peter, "Look! it is against our policy for God to allow this."

Peter answered, "Have you heard what John did just before he was put in prison? He and his men were hungry so he went to the bakery and ate the bread kept back for Herod. This happened when Stephen was a martyr.

"According to our Law, a priest cannot eat this food so John ate it all himself." Jesus began by saying, "Thursday was made for John, but John must not eat on Thursdays.

"The Father of man is Lord over every day."

2 *Find out:*
  (a) What does the word *sabbath* mean?
  (b) When does the Jewish sabbath begin and end?
  (c) What were the Pharisees accusing the disciples of when they picked the ears of corn and rubbed them in their hands?
  (d) Find out from a textbook and the Bible as much as you can about David, what he did as a boy, and his achievements in his later life.

3 *Opinion:*
  (a) Why do you think Jesus made reference to what David had done on the Sabbath?
  (b) When Jesus said, "The Sabbath is made for the good of man; man was not made for the Sabbath" did he mean that the Jewish laws were not important? Or did he mean that it is important to keep the general spirit of a religious law but not to be obsessed with the details? Or that some things are more important than keeping all the rules? *Discuss.*

4 *Research:*
Find out how others feel about the possibility of all shops and stores being able to open on a Sunday. *Write down* their views. Does this story give any guidance about it?

Mark 3.1–6

10: Jesus heals the man with a paralysed hand

Objectives

To show how anger toward Jesus led to a plot to kill him.

To learn of the attitude of the Jews to work on the Sabbath day.

To study the ways in which Jesus healed people.

1 Write a *newspaper report* of this miracle, after reading the passage from Mark. Mention where the miracle took place and how Jesus healed the man.

2 *Find out*:
  (a) What does the word *synagogue* mean?
  (b) What does *stubborn* mean?
  (c) How many people must be present in a synagogue before worship can begin? What kind of people must they be? How might women feel about this?

3 *Opinion*:
  (a) Which group of people do you think criticized Jesus? (Consider the work you have done in the past.)
  (b) Does this miracle story support the claim of Christians that Jesus is the Son of God?

  Write down the opinions given.

4 *Research*:
  (a) Why do you think some people showed anger toward Jesus and plotted to kill him? Conduct an opinion survey and ask for reasons. *Write down* the different views expressed.
  (b) Find out what you can about spiritual healing.
  (c) What was the method of healing used by Jesus? Make a grid (or use one you have already made) to compare all the healings you study in the gospels: Make *three* headings: *Place, Person healed, Method of healing*. Write in information about all the healings you have learnt about so far and then keep adding information to the grid when you read about others.

11: Peter's declaration at Caesarea Philippi

Assignment No.

Time allowed

Objectives

To show how some people felt about Jesus.

To find out what the term Messiah means.

To show that Jesus had plans for Peter.

To show that Jesus gave Peter special responsibilities.

1 *Complete these sentences* after reading the passage from Matthew:
  (a) Jesus went to the territory .... where he asked his disciples, "............ is?"
  (b) Jesus' disciples answered, "Some say ...., others say ...., while others say ...."
  (c) Simon Peter answered, "............ God."
  (d) Jesus said, "For this truth .... Father in heaven."
  (e) "I tell you, Peter: .... church and not even .... overcome it."
  (f) "I will give you the ....; what you prohibit .... prohibited in heaven."
  (g) Jesus ordered ....

2 *Join the word to the correct sentence:*

Word	Sentence
(a) John	means "a rock" in Greek.
(b) Elijah	baptized Jesus in the river Jordan.
(c) The Messiah	was the place where Peter made a declaration about Jesus.
(d) Jeremiah	is the Greek word meaning Messiah.
(e) Christ	was an important Jewish prophet.
(f) Peter	was an important Jewish prophet.
(g) Caesarea Philippi	was a saviour expected by the Jews (Hebrew word).

3 *Think about the story and answer:*
  (a) What was the important thing Simon Peter realized about Jesus?
  (b) What did Jesus say about Simon Peter, and what did he mean?
  (c) What do you think Jesus meant by "the keys of the Kingdom of heaven"?
  (d) Why did some people think that Jesus was John, Elijah or Jeremiah?
  (e) What do you think the disciples thought about Peter's declaration of faith?

4 *Opinion*:
What do people today think that Jesus was? Ask around until you have *five* different opinions to write down.

5 *Research*:
Draw a map of the Holy Land to keep in your folder. Mark on it the town of Caesarea Philippi.

LIFE AND TEACHING OF JESUS   **II · Positive and negative responses to Jesus**

Assignment No.

Time allowed

12: The Transfiguration of Jesus

Objectives

To learn about the events in the story of the transfiguration.

To consider whether the story may be helpful for followers of Jesus.

To note the words spoken about Jesus and the importance attached to them.

1 Write *a summary of the story* from Mark's Gospel. Mention what happened, the people present, and what was said.

2 *Find out*:
  (a) What does *transfiguration* mean?
  (b) After what other event in the life of Jesus are similar words spoken about him?
  (c) What do Moses and Elijah represent?
  (d) What indication is there in this story to suggest that the "chosen one" is to be a sacrifice for the sins of mankind?

3 *Opinion*:
  (a) Given that Jesus was "seen" with Moses and Elijah by three of his disciples, do you think this would have been important for his early followers? *Discuss* this and *write down* your views.
  (b) What is your explanation for the temporary change in Jesus' appearance?

4 *Research*:
  Find out from books and from asking people what kind of ways there may be to understand religious experiences and visions. Ask several people, quietly and in private, whether they have ever had a religious experience which they could not explain, and what it meant to them. *Write a paragraph* about this.

LIFE AND TEACHING OF JESUS   **II · Positive and negative responses to Jesus**

13: Jesus at the home of Simon the Pharisee

Objectives

To note that those who have done wrong in the past can have great love for Jesus.

To appreciate that all people can be forgiven.

To consider if this story offers hope for those who have done wrong.

1 Read the story from Luke's Gospel and *complete the following sentences*:
   (a) The name of the Pharisee who invited Jesus into his house was ....
   (b) The woman brought .... to the house.
   (c) The woman wet Jesus' feet with ....
   (d) The woman did the following *three* things to Jesus' feet: (1) ....
       (2) .... (3) ....
   (e) There were *three* things the Pharisee did not give Jesus when he entered his house.
       They were: (1) .... (2) .... (3) ....
   (f) The woman showed .... and this led Jesus to say, that her sins had been
       forgiven.
   (g) The people sitting at the table said, ...
   (h) .... had saved the woman.

2 *Opinion*:
   (a) What point was Jesus making when he told the story of the money-lender? *Write down*
       your ideas and ask others for their views.
   (b) Do you think there is evidence in the story to suggest that Jesus was aware of the
       thoughts of others?
   (c) Why do you think Simon the Pharisee reacted toward Jesus in the way he did? Look up
       this story in a textbook and *make a note* of your discoveries.

3 *Research*:
   How might Jesus' attitude toward the woman offer hope for people who have done wrong
   and feel concerned to "wipe the slate clean"? Ask people from a variety of age groups for
   their opinions. *Write down* their views along with your own.

LIFE AND TEACHING OF JESUS   II · Positive and negative responses to Jesus

Assignment No.	
Time allowed	

14 : Jesus visits Mary and Martha

Objectives

To show that Jesus is more concerned with responses to his teaching than the performance of everyday routine.

To note that some people are often concerned with the unimportant tasks in life.

To consider the qualities of the two women.

1 Read the story from Luke's Gospel carefully and *complete the following sentences:*
  (a) Jesus and his disciples were welcomed by . . . .
  (b) Martha had a sister named . . . . who sat down at . . . . and
      . . . . teaching.
  (c) . . . . was upset because of the . . . . she had to do.
  (d) Martha said, ... that my . . . . work? Tell her to come and
      . . . .
  (e) Jesus said to Martha . . . . things, but just one is . . . . and Mary has
      . . . . her.

2 *Find out:*
  (a) What do you think Jesus meant when he said ". . . but just one thing is needed. Mary has chosen the right thing. . . ."?
  (b) Some people would say that this story has a message that is worthwhile. What do you think it is? *Write a slogan* that you feel expresses the message.

3 *Opinion:*
  (a) Why do you think Jesus did not mind Martha doing all the housework? Do you think Jesus' attitude toward Martha was unfair? Write down your ideas.
  (b) How would you describe Mary and Martha? Make two headings: *Mary/Martha* and list the qualities you think apply to each one.
  (c) Which of the two characters is like you? Think about this question and say why you think so.

4 *Research:*
  (a) Do you think we spend too much time worrying about unnecessary and unimportant issues that arise in our lives?
  (b) Ask *ten* people of all ages to list the *six* most important issues that they are concerned with in their lives. Make a *bar chart* to show your findings.

Assignment No.
Time allowed

15 : Jesus and Zacchaeus

Objectives

To show that outcasts were also welcomed by Jesus to follow him and his teaching.

To find out the meaning of the word salvation. (It is connected with the word save.)

To consider who the "lost" are today.

1 After reading the passage from Luke's Gospel, *either*, write Zacchaeus' diary for the day; use the beginning of each sentence (*a*) to (*f*) below to help you:

(*a*) I heard that . . . .

(*b*) To get a better view I . . . .

(*c*) I never expected . . . .

(*d*) When he said that he was coming to my house I was worried because . . . .

(*e*) While Jesus was with me I realized . . . .

(*f*) I decided . . . .

Or

Complete the following sentences:

(*g*) Zacchaeus . . . . a tree so that he could . . . .

(*h*) Jesus said to the tax collector, ". . . . . because I . . . . stay . . . . today."

(*i*) Zacchaeus . . . . down and . . . . joy.

(*j*) The people grumbled when . . . . went into the . . . . collector's house because . . . .

(*k*) The tax collector said he would give . . . . of his . . . . to the . . . .

2 *Find out*:

(*a*) Why were tax collectors hated and treated as outcasts? (There is a clue in the story.)

(*b*) What does the word *salvation* mean?

(*c*) Which tax collector became a disciple of Jesus?

3 *Opinion*:

(*a*) Why do you think some tax collectors were against Jesus and his teaching? *Write down your views.*

(*b*) Jesus said: "The son of Man came to seek and to save!" Which people do you think Jesus would seek and try to save if he returned to earth tomorrow?

(*c*) In this story Zacchaeus' change of heart was good news for a lot of people; who?

(*d*) Do you think salvation is something that affects one person, or something that affects the whole community?

LIFE AND TEACHING OF JESUS   **II · Positive and negative responses to Jesus**

Assignment No.
Time allowed

16 : Discipleship

Objectives

To encourage an understanding of the problems, hardships and rewards of being a disciple of Jesus.

To analyse why some people rejected Jesus and the disciples.

1 Make *two columns*, one headed *Problems and Hardships* and the other headed *Rewards and Advantages*.

Read the six passages, and as you read each one try to spot the problems and rewards of being a disciple and write them in the columns. There is an example below:

Problems and Hardships	Rewards and Advantages
Leaving the family.	Being able to heal people.

2 *Find out*:
   (a) Write *six* sentences explaining what you have discovered from the *six* passages.
   (b) Which women followed Jesus?
   (c) Why would the people of Samaria not see Jesus? Mark Samaria on your map.
   (d) What did Jesus mean when he said, "Foxes have holes and birds have nests"?
   (e) Jesus said, "Let the dead bury their own dead". What did Jesus mean by this?
   (f) What were the disciples able to do that showed they had power over the enemy?
   (g) What did Jesus mean when he said to the seventy-two, "There is a large harvest but few workers to gather it in"?
   (h) Who are the wolves?
   (i) Why do you think Jesus gave the disciples the instruction not to move around from house to house?
   (j) What action were the disciples to perform in a town that did not welcome them?
   (k) What was Sodom? Why did Jesus refer to it? Use a Bible dictionary to help you.

3 *Opinion*:
Why do you think some people were not prepared to listen to the preaching of the disciples? Write down your views.

LIFE AND TEACHING OF JESUS   **II · Positive and negative responses to Jesus**

Text © Andrew Lawrence 1990. Illustration © Richard Smith 1990
Multiple copies of this sheet may be made by the purchasing institution only.

Assignment No.	
Time allowed	

17 : The Good Samaritan

Objectives

To show how Jesus used people as examples in his teaching.

To appreciate the deeper meaning of the story and the importance of this for today.

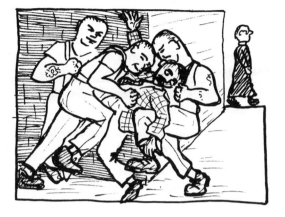

1 Read the story of the Good Samaritan from Luke and *write a newspaper report* including the following words:

> *attacked, innkeeper, oil, pity, Levite, inn, silver, care, animal, coins, neighbour, bandaged, Jericho, priest, wine, Samaritan, robbers, Jerusalem, wounds.*

It may also help you to begin by thinking out the various characters and the setting before you start.

2 *Find out*:
 (a) Find out which *two* of the ten commandments are mentioned in this parable and write them down.
 (b) What was the job of a Levite? Look up the word *Levite* in the index of a textbook for information.
 (c) Use a textbook; try to find out how some Jews felt about the people from Samaria (Samaritans). Write a short paragraph saying why they felt the way they did.
 (d) What does the man from Samaria (the Samaritan) represent in this story?
 (e) Was the Samaritan a Jew or a Gentile?

3 *Opinion*:
Has this story got anything to teach us about how to live today? Think of a situation that could arise in our country now which is similar to that in the story and tell the story in a modern setting.

4 *Research*:
Find out as much as you can about the Samaritans organization in your area. Write a short *magazine article* about it.

Assignment No.	
Time allowed	

18: The Rich Fool (The Rich Man and His Barns)

Objectives

To learn that many people are only concerned for themselves.

To show Jesus' attitude toward accumulation of too much wealth.

To consider whether Jesus' teaching has any relevance in today's world.

To learn where true wealth is to be found, according to Jesus' teaching.

1 Write your own *summary* of the story in Luke's Gospel, explain what the man did and his reason for doing so. Mention why the man was a fool.

2 *Find out*:
What did Jesus say about the difficulties the "rich" may have in trying to enter the kingdom of God/heaven? (See Luke 18.18–30.)

3 *Opinion*:
(a) What do you think Jesus meant when he said, "A person's true life is not made up of the things he owns, no matter how rich he may be"?
(b) How can a person become "rich" in God's sight?
(c) Write a simple sentence that you think sums up this story.
(d) What evidence is there in this story that suggests that the man took life for granted? Write down your views in a few sentences.

4 *Research*:
(a) Is there a lesson to be learned in this story that might help us in our materialistic world today? Ask others this question and write down their comments. Make a *simple chart* to show the responses you found.
(b) Look at a few recent newspapers for examples where possessions, money and wealth are given great importance.
Make *two columns*, like the ones below, with headings and list your findings.

Title, theme, name of article	*What is it about/saying?*

(c) What do you think Jesus would say to rich people today?
(d) Choose an organization today that helps people who are poor, such as Oxfam, Christian Aid, Band Aid, Shelter, Save the Children. *Write a short article* describing it and saying why you think people who are well off should support it.

LIFE AND TEACHING OF JESUS   **III · Parables told by Jesus**

Assignment No.	
Time allowed	

19: The Pharisee and the Tax Collector

Objectives

To show that many of the Pharisees were not as close to God as those they despised.

To show Jesus' attitude toward those who thought they were more God-fearing than others.

To consider what lessons there are in the parable that could be of help to us today.

1 After reading the parable from Luke's Gospel, *make three columns*, like the ones below, read the story and write down in the appropriate column what each man said and what kind of people they were.

Person	What did he say?	What kind of person was he?
The Pharisee		
The tax collector		

2 *Find out*:
   (a) What does the word *humble* mean?
   (b) What did Jesus mean when he said, "Everyone who makes himself great will be humbled, and everyone who humbles himself will be made great"?

3 *Opinion*:
   (a) Are there any people who you think are better than you are? Who?
   (b) Are there any people who you think are worse than you are? Who?
   (c) The Pharisees were so proud they always kept to the traditional rules and the Law. Do you think that laws, rules and commandments may get in the way of a person's attempt to get closer to God and other people? *Write down* your ideas and give reasons for your views.

4 *Research*:
Ask people from different age groups to read your summary of the story and then to answer your questions:
   (a) Have you ever been like the Pharisee?
   (b) What do you think of the basic message of this story?

Write down their opinions.

LIFE AND TEACHING OF JESUS   **III · Parables told by Jesus**

20: The Ten Bridesmaids

Objectives

To learn of Jesus' teaching about being ready to receive him.

To be prepared and ready for the unexpected in everyday living.

To show Jesus' attitude toward those who were not prepared for the unexpected.

To learn about the idea of the Second Coming.

1 After reading the parable in Matthew, *write a newspaper report* headlined: "Five Bridesmaids Miss Wedding".

2 *Find out*:
  (a) What does "they *trimmed* their lamps" mean?
  (b) Who is the bridegroom in the parable?
  (c) What do the symbols oil and light represent? Use a textbook or a Bible dictionary to find the information.
  (d) What does Jesus mean when he says: "Be on your guard then, because you do not know the day or the hour"? Use a textbook to answer this question.

3 *Opinion*:
  (a) In not more than *ten* words, write down what you think the message of this story is.
  (b) How do you think the bridesmaids who missed the bridegroom felt?
  (c) How did the others feel who were ready?
  (d) From what you have studied, were there people who were ready for Jesus and his teaching? Which people were they?
  (e) Were there people who were not ready for Jesus and this teaching?
  (f) If Jesus came back soon and appeared where you live, who would be pleased to see him, and who might not be pleased? How would you feel?

4 *Research*:
  In order to find out and write about belief in the Second Coming of Christ, choose one of the following activities:
  (a) Study passages in the Gospels and your textbook about the Second Coming of Christ and *write down* what you think they are saying.
  (b) Find out the meaning of these words: *advent, millennium, apocalypse*.
  (c) Find out what Jehovah's Witnesses, Adventists or other religious groups believe about the Second Coming.

Assignment No.	
Time allowed	

21 : The Sower

Objectives

To develop an understanding of Jesus' use of symbols in his teaching.

To try to encourage analysis of Jesus' teaching in a search for deeper meaning.

To consider what lessons there are in the parable that could be of practical help to us today.

1 Read the parable and *write a simple account* of what was said by Jesus.

2 *Find out*:
(a) Make *three* columns like the ones below.

Item	Represents in the time of Jesus	Represents today
The Sower		
The Seed		
The Rock		
The Birds		

Read the story carefully and try to find *three* other items for your list. Put these in the item column and discuss what each may have represented in the time of Jesus. Do the items represent anything different today?

(b) What is Jesus' message in this parable? How important might this story be for Christians today? *Write a short paragraph* giving your views.

3 *Research*:
What factors today make people unwilling to follow the teaching of Jesus?
What factors make people want to know about it?
Ask several people what they think and why, and make *two columns* showing the factors for and against.

Text © Andrew Lawrence 1990. Illustration © Richard Smith 1990
Multiple copies of this sheet may be made by the purchasing institution only.

Luke 15.1–7; 15.8–10; 15.11–32

22: The Lost Son, Sheep and Coin

Objectives

To learn that these three parables have a common message.

To show that the Kingdom of God/heaven is for all people.

To show that these parables offer hope for mankind today.

To learn the meaning of "lost" in the parables.

1 Read the parable of the lost sheep and *complete the following sentences*:
  (a) A man had . . . . sheep, he . . . . one so he . . . . the other . . . . in the pasture.
  (b) He went looking for . . . . got . . . .
  (c) When he found . . . . shoulders . . . . home.
  (d) He then called his friends . . . . and said, "I'm . . . . celebrate!"
  (e) In the same way there will be more joy in . . . . over one . . . . who repents than over . . . . people who do not need to . . . .

2 *Find out*:
  (a) What did the Pharisees and the Teachers of the Law say to Jesus that caused him to tell the story of the lost sheep?
  (b) In the story of the lost son, which son wanted his share of the property?
  (c) What job did the son take and what did he wish he could eat?
  (d) What did the son decide he would say when he returned home to his father?
  (e) What happens in all *three* parables when the lost is found?
  (f) What does the word *repent* mean?
  (g) Who do the shepherd, the woman and the father in these three parables represent?
  (h) The phrase "God is love" can be seen in these parables. Can you explain how?

3 *Opinion*:
  (a) What do these parables tell us about God?
  (b) Is there evidence to suggest that the father of the lost son had been looking out for him for a long time and that he did not want his son to have to beg to be taken back into the family? What does this say about God's relationship with people?
  (c) Which group of people, in the time of Jesus, might be like the older brother? (Look at verse 28 of the story and also verse 2 of the story of the Lost Sheep.)
  (d) Write *two* or *three* sentences to sum up the attitude of the elder brother; and *two* or *three* sentences to say how the younger brother felt. Which one is more like you? Discuss this with your friends and *write down* how they felt.
  (e) Do you think the story of the lost son would help parents to cope with the problems caused by their teenage son/daughter who has got into trouble for the first time? Think about the attitude of the father in the story. Write a *brief summary* of your ideas.

23 : The Mustard Seed and the Yeast

Objectives

To show the Kingdom of heaven grows slowly from small beginnings.

To show that the Kingdom of God offers "support" for all.

1 *Complete the following sentences* from the parables of the mustard seed and the yeast.
  (a) The Kingdom of heaven is like this. A man . . . . It is the smallest of all seeds, but when . . . . It becomes a tree, so that . . . .
  (b) Jesus told them still another parable: the Kingdom of . . . . A woman takes some yeast . . . .

2 *Find out*:
  (a) Who is the man who sows the seeds?
  (b) What do the seed and yeast represent?
  (c) Who might the birds in the parable represent?
  (d) What is the simple message of these two short parables?

3 *Opinion*:
  (a) Do you think an idea or belief of a few people can grow to change the world? Can you think of any examples?
  (b) What would you say to someone who says it's not worth doing anything about the world's problems because they are too big?
  (c) Do you think the disciples of Jesus ever felt discouraged?

4 *Research*:
  Choose a person such as Gandhi, Florence Nightingale or William Wilberforce, who managed to change attitudes, and tell their story *in your own words*.

| Assignment No. |
| Time allowed |

24 : The Hidden Treasure and the Pearl

Objectives

To appreciate that the Kingdom of God often lies hidden.

To understand that great sacrifices have to be made in order to gain entry into the Kingdom of God and that such sacrifice is worthwhile according to Christian belief.

1 After reading the parables, copy out the passage below and *fill in the missing words.*
   (a) The Kingdom of . . . . is like this. A man . . . . to find a . . . . hidden in a . . . . He . . . . it up again and is so . . . . that he goes back and . . . . everything he has, and then goes back and . . . . that field.
   (b) Now, complete the story of the pearl:
   The Kingdom of heaven is like this. A man is looking . . . . unusually fine, ... sells . . . . has . . . . pearl.

2 *Opinion*:
   (a) What do the hidden treasure and the pearl represent?
   (b) How do we know that what has been found is valuable?
   (c) Ask *three* friends if there is anything really valuable they would like to get in their lives, and whether they would make sacrifices to get it. Note their answers.

3 *Research*:
Write *in your own words* a real or imaginary news item about someone who made sacrifices for something they believed was valuable.

LIFE AND TEACHING OF JESUS   **III · Parables told by Jesus**

Assignment No.

Time allowed

25: The Weeds and the Net

Objectives

To show that the followers of Jesus lived in a world where they often encountered evil.

To try to understand the use of symbols in the stories.

To consider the idea of judgement.

1 Read the two parables carefully and *see how many key words you can list* in the left-hand column. There are possibly *ten* words you could list. What do you think each of the key words represents?

(Leave adequate space between each key word.)

Key Word	Represents
Wheat	
Weeds	
Fish	

2 *Opinion*:
   (a) Is it sometimes difficult to sort out in the real world who is good and who is bad? Why?
   (b) Who separated the wheat from the weeds in the story? What are these stories telling us about who should be the judge?
   (c) Do these stories give the impression that Jesus is saying that hell exists? Do you think that ideas about burning in hell come from the story about the wheat and the weeds?
   (d) What do you think about heaven and hell?

3 *Research*:
   Either study the work of artists to see how they thought about hell,

   or find out what another religion such as Islam teaches about heaven and hell.

   or make a *survey* of ten people's views on heaven and hell and *write it up.*

| Assignment No. |
| Time allowed |

26: The Three Servants

Objectives

To learn that being a follower of Jesus required much effort and personal sacrifice and that the same is true for Christians today.

To consider the skills we have and to use them in all we attempt rather than give up before trying.

1 After reading the parable carefully, *make three columns*, like the ones below, *and put on the headings*. Read the story of the three servants and *fill in the columns* for each one.

Servant	How much was given?	What was done with the money?	What was finally given to each servant?
First			
Second			
Third			

2 *Find out*:
   (a) What does *investment* mean? (Use a dictionary if you need to.)
   (b) What is the parable really about? Is it about making money, or is there a deeper meaning to be found in it?

3 *Opinion*:
   (a) Write down a simple slogan that sums up this story.
   (b) What do the amounts of money in the story represent? *Write a few lines* to explain.
   (c) Do you think the master was unnecessarily cruel to the servant who buried the thousand coins? *Write down* your views, giving reasons.
   (d) What talents do you think you have? What do you think you should do to develop those talents?

Assignment No.

Time allowed

27 : Jesus calms a storm

Objectives

To understand the meaning of the miracle.

To appreciate the symbolism in the miracle.

To research the importance of the miracle for Christians today.

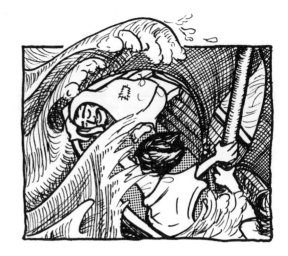

1 Read the story from Mark and *complete the following sentences:*
  (a) Jesus said to his disciples . . . .
  (b) So they left the crowd and the disciples got into . . . .
  (c) Other boats were . . . .
  (d) Suddenly a strong wind . . . .
  (e) Jesus was in the back . . . .
  (f) Jesus stood up and . . . .
  (g) Then Jesus said to his disciples . . . .
  (h) But they were terribly afraid . . . .

2 *Find out*:
  (a) Try to find out from a textbook the name of the lake or sea on which this event took place. Make sure it is marked on your map in your folder.
  (b) What is the meaning of the story? Use a textbook to help you discuss your views and then *write them down.*

3 *Opinion*:
  (a) Do you think people today find it difficult to believe in miracles? Discuss this and say how you feel.
  (b) Do you think people in Jesus' time were more likely to believe in him because of miracles? Do you think that miracles have the same effect today, or do they make it harder for people to believe?

LIFE AND TEACHING OF JESUS   IVA · **Jesus' miracles: Nature miracles**

Assignment No.
Time allowed

28 : Jesus walks on water

Objectives

To develop a greater understanding of the miracle.

To analyse the importance of the miracle for Christians today.

1 Read the story carefully. Imagine you see a newspaper reporter and you have just interviewed the disciples about this event. *Write a brief article for your newspaper.* The following questions may help you with your account: What happened? What was said? What changes took place?

2 *Find out*:
   (a) Which town is mentioned in the story? (Add it to your map.)
   (b) What did Jesus do immediately after the disciples left him to row across the lake?
   (c) Why did the disciples find it hard to row the boat?
   (d) Was it morning or afternoon when Jesus walked on the water?
   (e) Did the disciples believe in ghosts?
   (f) What happened in Matthew's story (14.27–33) that is not included in this account?

3 *Opinion*:
   (a) Discuss this miracle and try to discover what possible lesson could be learned from it. Write your views in a letter to a friend explaining the meaning that lies behind the story.
   (b) How might the miracle story support the view that Jesus was the Son of God? Write a *short summary* explaining your ideas.

4 *Research*:
   Find a book or article, or something in a textbook or encyclopaedia, about science and religion. Write *a paragraph* about this subject.

Assignment No.

Time allowed

29: Jesus feeds five thousand

Objectives

To consider in what other way the people could have been fed by Jesus.

To study other feeding stories and note any similarities and differences.

To show that Jesus was popular with many people.

1 After reading the story, imagine you were one of the 5,000 people that were fed by Jesus. *Write a short story*, in not more than 100 words, describing what happened that day.

2 *Find out*:
   (a) How did Jesus bless the bread?
   (b) What names are given to the present-day church service in which people are also "fed"?

3 *Opinion*:
   (a) What evidence is there in this story that shows Jesus and the disciples were popular?
   (b) What do you think Jesus meant when he said, "Sheep without a shepherd"?

4 *Research*:
   (a) Look up the Old Testament book of Exodus (chapter 16). How is this story similar?
   (b) Compare the feeding of the 5,000 with the feeding of the 4,000 and the meal in the upper room – the Last Supper.

Make a grid, like the one below, so that you are able to compare each account.

	Similarities	*Differences*
Feeding 5,000		
Feeding 4,000		
The Last Supper		

Think about what Jesus says and does in these three feeding stories before you write in your information.

30 : Jesus heals a man with evil spirits

Objectives

To show that Jesus had power over evil.

To show that Jesus was sympathetic and felt compassion toward mankind.

1 Read the story and *complete the following sentences*:
  (a) This miracle took place in the territory of ....
  (b) The man with evil spirits lived ....
  (c) The people tried to *restrain* the man with the evil spirits by ....
  (d) The man cut himself with ....
  (e) The man with the evil spirits said to Jesus ....
  (f) The man's name was ....
  (g) Jesus cast the evil spirits into ....
  (h) The man who was rid of the evil spirits said to Jesus as he began to leave ....
  (i) Jesus' instruction to the man was ....

2 *Opinion*:
How might the man's reaction be compared to that of Levi (Matthew)?

3 *Research*:
  (a) Find out about attitudes to mental illness today; *either* read articles and make a short summary of what you learn; *or* survey ten people's views as to whether the kind of illness described in the story is caused by demons, or whether it has some other cause. Write up your findings.
  (b) Mark the places you have read about on your map.

31: Jairus' daughter and the woman who touched Jesus' cloak

Objectives

To develop greater understanding of the miracles.

To consider if the miracles are important for Christians today.

1 Read the story carefully. Imagine you were an eye witness to the happenings in these stories and *write a brief summary of what you saw*:
  (a) Before Jesus arrived at Jairus' house.
  (b) When Jesus went inside Jairus' house.

2 *Complete the following sentences*:
  (a) For . . . . years the woman suffered . . . .
  (b) The woman said to herself . . . .
  (c) . . . . stopped the woman from bleeding.
  (d) Jesus knew that . . . . out of him.
  (e) Jesus said . . . . had made the woman well.
  (f) The messengers came to Jesus and said, ...
  (g) . . . . went into the house with Jesus.
  (h) When he had entered the house, Jesus said, ... The others . . . . at him.
  (i) As he took the girl's hand, Jesus said, ...
  (j) The girl was . . . . years old.
  (k) Jesus told them not to . . . .

3 *Opinions*:
  (a) Do these miracles show that Jesus had power over all things? Write a *brief statement* of your ideas.
  (b) These miracle stories must have been important for those who followed Jesus. Do you think they are important for Christians today? *Write down* your views.

| Assignment No. |
| Time allowed |

32: A woman's faith
(The Phoenician woman's daughter)

Objectives

To show that Jesus has power over all things and can heal.

To learn the hidden message of the conversation.

To show that outcasts were aware of Jesus' message and mission.

1 After reading the story, *make two columns*, like the ones below. *List the words that were said by Jesus and the woman*:

Words said by Jesus	Words said by the woman

2 *Find out*:
  (a) Try to work out how far the town in this story is from the place where Jesus lived as a boy, and where he was crucified. Use an atlas to help you.
  (b) What made the woman expect Jesus to reject her?
  (c) Which groups of people do you think the "children" and the "dogs" are in this story? Think of all the people Jesus mixed with.

3 *Opinion*:
  (a) What does the woman's reply to Jesus show about her *acceptance of him* and her *faith*?
  (b) What did the woman's answer show that made Jesus heal her child? Add the name of the miracle and the method of healing to the grid you made previously.
  (c) Do you think that people today show any prejudice or hostility toward foreigners, or people who are different from themselves? *Discuss* this and *record* your findings.

4 *Research*:
Bring your map up to date by adding in all the places you have read about.

Mark 10.46–52

33: Blind Bartimaeus

Objectives

To show that Jesus had power over all things and could also heal those with sense deficiencies.

To show that outcasts were pitied and healed by Jesus.

1 After reading the story, *complete these sentences*:
   (a) .... was the name of the man who was healed.
   (b) .... is the name of the city mentioned in this miracle.
   (c) The healing took place ....
   (d) The man called Jesus ....

2 *Find out*:
   (a) David is mentioned in the story. Who was he and why is Jesus called, "Son of David"?
   (b) Find out what the prefix "Bar" of the name Bartimaeus means. You may find the information in a Bible dictionary.
   (c) What evidence is there that suggests that the blind man became a disciple of Jesus in addition to the original twelve? (Remember disciple = follower.)
   (d) What did the man have that helped him to see again?

3 *Research*:
   Even though the man was blind, he knew who Jesus was – he could "see" in his mind's eye more than some people could with sight.

   From the work you have done previously, think about the following questions:
   (a) Who were the "blind" people who lived in Jesus' time? *Write down* your ideas.
   (b) Which people would you consider to be blind today?

   Look at recent newspapers for *three* different articles that show how some people, although they have sight, are in fact blind. You decide what you mean by "blind".

   Cut out only those articles that you feel are in keeping with your ideas. Stick them on paper.

   Write *three short summaries* saying why you have chosen them.

Assignment No.

Time allowed

34 : The Roman officer's servant
(The centurion's servant)

Objectives

To show that those who are regarded as sinners and outcasts often have the greater faith.

To show that Jesus has power over all things and can heal.

To show that not all the Romans were oppressive toward the Jews.

To assess the character of the soldier.

To show that outcasts were aware of Jesus' message and mission.

HE SAYS, JUST GIVE THE ORDER

1 Read the story carefully and *write the endings to these sentences*:
   (a) Jesus went to a town known as ....
   (b) A Roman soldier had a ....
   (c) When the officer heard about ....
   (d) They came to Jesus and ....
   (e) "The Roman soldier really deserves your ...."
   (f) "He loves our people and ...."
   (g) When Jesus was fairly near the house ....
   (h) "Just give the order," said the soldier, "and my ...."
   (i) "I too am a man ...."
   (j) Jesus was surprised when he heard ....
   (k) The messengers went back to ....

2 *Find out*:
   (a) The Roman officer is sometimes known as a *centurion*. Find out why. (Use a dictionary if you have any problems.)
   (b) The soldier was a Roman and therefore not a Jew: find out the Jewish name for non-Jews (it starts with G). Would Jews enter the houses of non-Jews?
   (c) Why did the messengers take so much trouble to help the soldier?
   (d) Having learnt the meaning of the word humility already, *write down* the words of *humility* expressed by the soldier.
   (e) What actually cured the servant?
   (f) What evidence in the story suggests that not all the Jewish elders were against Jesus or too proud to approach him for help?
   (g) Use a Bible atlas to find where the town mentioned is situated. Put the town on the map you have developed previously.

3 *Opinion*:
   (a) What words can you list to show the type of person the soldier was?
   (b) Do you think Jesus thought the soldier was an extraordinary person? *Write down* your views in a brief paragraph.
   (c) What was the method of healing used by Jesus? Add this to your grid previously started.

LIFE AND TEACHING OF JESUS   **IVB · Jesus' miracles: Healing miracles**

Assignment No.
Time allowed

35: Jesus heals ten men

Objectives

To show that Jesus has power over all things and can heal whenever and wherever he wishes.

To show that outcasts were aware of who Jesus was and his power.

To discover something of Jewish attitudes toward diseases and sin.

To continue building up information showing how Jesus healed.

To consider who are often regarded as inferior in today's world.

1 *Find out:*
   Answer the questions after reading the story:
   (a) What do we call the disease that the men may have been suffering from?
   (b) What did the men say to Jesus?
   (c) Who were to examine the men?
   (d) Being a foreigner, a non-Jew, the man was regarded as a: ....
      (Finish the sentence.)
   (e) What had made the men well again?
      Add this miracle and the method of healing to your grid.
   (f) The men with the disease were regarded as outcasts. Why was this?
      Try to find out from a textbook what the Jews felt about disease and sin.

2 *Opinion:*
   Why do you think it was mentioned that the man who thanked Jesus was a foreigner?
   Write down your ideas and discuss this with others.

3 *Research:*
   Choose any one group of people who might be regarded as outcasts today, or who suffer some kind of hostility or prejudice. Study their situation and the reasons for it, and find out what is being done to solve this problem. The group you choose might be victims of racial or sexual discrimination, or sufferers from AIDS or mental or physical disability.

LIFE AND TEACHING OF JESUS

IVB · Jesus' miracles: Healing miracles

| Assignment No. |
| Time allowed |

36 : Jesus raises a widow's son
(The widow of Nain's son)

Objectives

To show the human nature of Jesus in this miracle.

To develop basic mapwork skills.

To discover something of Jewish burial customs.

To analyse our own thoughts regarding the miracles.

1 After reading the story from Luke, *write a brief summary* explaining where Jesus was and what he saw and said to help the widow.

2 *Mapwork*:
Find the town mentioned in a Bible atlas. Put the town mentioned in this story on the map you made. Also, put in three other towns that are nearby.

3 *Find out*:
Use an atlas to help you with the following:
(a) In which region is the town mentioned?
(b) Name a mountain near the place where this miracle took place.
(c) List three towns that are near Nain.
(d) Estimate the distance between Nain and the Mediterranean Sea.
(e) Why might some people feel very sorry for the woman?
(f) Why do you think the people said: "God has come to save his people!"?
(*Discuss* and then *write down* your ideas.)
(g) How did Jesus raise the boy to life? Add the method of healing in this story to your grid.

4 *Opinion*:
(a) How does this miracle show the human side of Jesus? *Write down* your ideas.
(b) What are your views of Jesus' healings?

How would you respond to someone who said: "All the miracle stories were made up and it is pointless to believe in them"?

Think about this question carefully, ask others for their views. Make *a report* of your findings.

5 *Research*:
What do the Jews do with people when they die? Look in a textbook for information. *Write down* what you have found out about funeral customs.

| Assignment No. |
| Time allowed |

37 : Triumphant entry into Jerusalem
(Palm Sunday)

Objectives

To learn of the occasion when Jesus entered into Jerusalem, which marked the beginning of the last week before he was crucified.

To examine the importance of this event. Why did all the Gospel writers include it?

1 Read the story carefully and *complete the following sentences*:
  (a) Jesus sent the disciples ahead of him, saying, ...
  (b) If you are asked why you are untying the colt, tell them, ...
  (c) They found the colt just as Jesus had said. As they were untying it, its owners said,
      . . . .
  (d) "The . . . . needs it," they answered.
  (e) They took . . . . to Jesus.
  (f) They threw their . . . . and helped Jesus get on.
  (g) As Jesus rode . . . . on the road.
  (h) When he was near . . . . at the place where . . . . down the mount of
      . . . . the large . . . . began to thank and praise him in loud voices for all
      . . . .
  (i) ". . . . . who comes in the name of the . . . . Peace in . . . . to
      God!"

2 *Opinion*:
  (a) What do you think that putting cloaks and branches on the road before Jesus says about how some people felt about him?
  (b) This event marks the beginning of the last week of Jesus' life. Do you think:
      (i) Jesus knew he was going to die? (See Luke 18.31–34.)
          If so, why did he not turn around and go elsewhere?
      (ii) The people knew what was going to happen to Jesus within a week of arriving in Jerusalem?

Write down your views.

3 *Research*:
  Find out about the city of Jerusalem in the time of Jesus; who ruled it? Find a map of the city and note where the Temple was and where the Roman soldiers were. Try to find Gethsemane and Golgotha (where the crucifixion took place). Draw *a plan* to refer to in the next few units.

LIFE AND TEACHING OF JESUS

V · Jesus' last week on Earth

Assignment No.

Time allowed

38: Jesus goes into the Temple

Objectives

To show Jesus' attitude toward misuse of God's Temple.

To show the true character of the chief priests and teachers of the Law.

To think about the value of a "house of prayer" in the community today.

1 Read the story carefully. *Find the errors* in the following passage and *rewrite it correctly*:

> When they arrived in Bethlehem, Peter went with Jesus into a synagogue and found five loaves and two fish on a table beside the stools of the pigeon fanciers. Jesus was unhappy that many people were selling fish in God's house of prayer. Jesus said, "It is written in the temple, that the synagogue is God's place of rest and you thieves are working here and on the Sabbath day."
> The lawyers who were watching were unhappy and thought of a way to get even with Jesus, even though everyone else thought he was a good man.

2 *Find out*:
Did Jesus stay overnight in the city?

3 *Opinion*:
  (a) Do you think this event had any influence on the attitudes of the chief priests and lawyers?
  (b) Did Jesus lose his temper or was he angry? What is the difference? *Write down* your views.
  (c) What can we learn from the words spoken by Jesus?

4 *Research*:
  (a) Do you think that "God's house" is an important building to have in the community?
  (b) If there were suddenly no religious buildings in your community, would something special be lost?
  (c) Why do many non-churchgoers want to get married in a church? Ask as many people as possible for their views on these three questions.

Present your findings using a *bar chart* or any other suitable form. You may wish to discuss what is meant by *God's house* and also the findings of your survey.

LIFE AND TEACHING OF JESUS

V · Jesus' last week on Earth

Assignment No.	
Time allowed	

39 : The question about Jesus' authority

Objectives

To learn of Jesus' powerful use of argument and thought.

To develop an awareness of the growing anger of some of the Jewish officials toward Jesus.

To learn of the special qualities that Jesus had.

1 Make a *brief summary* of the story from Mark's Gospel explaining where the conversation took place, what was said to Jesus, and Jesus' reply.

2 *Find out*:
  (a) Why were the men "tongue-tied"? (Why could they not answer Jesus?)
  (b) Why might the chief priests, lawyers and elders be angry toward Jesus?

3 *Opinion*:
  What makes a person special or outstanding amongst others?
  Ask others this simple question and *write down* their opinions.
  What is the main opinion given?

4 *Research*:
  (a) Look in a recent newspaper for a picture of someone who you think is special. *Write down three* reasons why you feel the way you do.
  (b) What reasons do you think some people would give for their opinion that Jesus was a very special person? If you find this difficult, ask others for their opinions.

LIFE AND TEACHING OF JESUS   **V · Jesus' last week on Earth**

Text © Andrew Lawrence 1990. Illustration © Richard Smith 1990

Assignment No.
Time allowed

40: The parable of the Tenants in the Vineyard

Objectives

To learn of Jesus' attitude toward the religious leaders.

To show the true character of the chief priests and teachers of the Law.

To consider how Jesus regarded himself and his purpose on earth.

To understand the use of symbolism.

1 *Find out the meaning* of these words from the story (use a dictionary if you need to):

winepress, vineyard, tenants, seized, shamefully.

2 Write a *short summary* of the story saying where the story takes place, what happened to the slaves and the owner's son. What were Jesus' words?

3 *Find out*:
  (a) What would the grapes be used for other than for eating?
  (b) Make *two columns* with headings, like the ones below. Put in all the people mentioned in the story. Think about what each represents and put your ideas in the column.

Character or thing	Represents
The man	
The slaves	
The son	
The tenants who killed	
The other tenants Jesus spoke of who would eventually have the vineyard	
The vineyard	

  (c) Explain why this story angered the chief priests and lawyers.
  (d) Who were the builders? (Mark 12.10.) Do you think all those who were listening to the story were "builders" in the manner that Jesus used this term in the story? *Discuss* and *write down* your ideas.
  (e) From which Old Testament book does the following scripture come from?

  The stone which the builders rejected as worthless turned out to be the most important of all.

4 *Opinion*:
  (a) What does this story tell us about human nature? *Write down* your ideas and the ideas of four other people.
  (b) Why do you think the tenants behaved in the way they did?

Assignment No.
Time allowed

41: The question about paying taxes

Objectives

To learn of Jesus' attitude toward God and the state authority.

To show the relationship which existed between Jesus and the Pharisees.

To consider if there is a message in the story that is helpful for today.

1 *Make a summary of the story*, explaining how some people tried to trap Jesus, and Jesus' responses to them.

2 *Find out*:
  (a) Who was the Roman Emperor when Jesus began his ministry? See Luke's Gospel, chapter 3.
  (b) Why were Roman coins used in Jesus' country?

3 *Opinion*:
  (a) "............ pay God what belongs to God". What do you think Jesus meant by this statement?
  (b) How would you react if your town or country was conquered and ruled by people from another country? *Write down* your views.
  (c) What worthwhile advice does this story offer? *Write down* your ideas.
  (d) The passage describes the question put to Jesus by the Pharisees as a "trick". How was it a trick and what were the Pharisees trying to achieve?

4 *Research*:
Look up the section on the Zealots in your textbook and try to find out what they felt about Roman occupation of their land. You may have to ask your teacher for help.

If the Zealots overheard Jesus' answer: "Pay the Emperor what belongs to the Emperor and pay God what belongs to God", how do you think they might have reacted?

LIFE AND TEACHING OF JESUS   V · Jesus' last week on Earth

| Assignment No. |
| Time allowed |

42: Jesus warns against teachers of the Law

Objectives

To note Jesus' warnings about the teachers of the Law.

To discover the true character of many of the teachers of the Law.

1 After reading the passage from Mark, *make a list* of all the things Jesus accused the teachers of the Law of committing.

2 *Find out*:
(a) What was the occupation of a teacher of the Law in the time of Jesus?
(b) From the information you have gained already, describe how many of the teachers of the Law felt about Jesus. Give examples of their feelings and attitudes toward Jesus to support your answer. You may wish to use the index of a textbook for additional information about the teachers of the Law.

3 *Opinion*:
Discuss and then *write two lists*: one setting out the advantages of having rules for behaviour and keeping them; the other list should show the disadvantages of making these rules too important or too rigid.

4 *Research*:
From a newspaper, try to find present-day examples that show people who behave like the teachers of the Law. Cut out and stick the cuttings into your folder.

LIFE AND TEACHING OF JESUS   **V · Jesus' last week on Earth**

Assignment No.	
Time allowed	

43 : The widow's offering
(widow's mite)

Objectives

To learn of Jesus' teaching on wealth.

To give thought to the importance of Jesus' teaching for Christians today.

1 *Make a summary* of this story and mention where it took place.

2 Make *two columns* with headings like the ones below.
List all the people mentioned and *write down* what each represents. Ask others for their views also.

Person	Represents
The rich people	
The poor widow	
The disciples	

3 *Find out*:
What did Jesus say about the difficulties the rich would have in gaining entry into the Kingdom of heaven? (See Luke 18.24–25.)

4 *Opinion*:
(a) In what way did the widow give more than the rich people?
(b) What reasons might rich people give to show why they could not give more?

5 *Research*:
Can a millionaire be a Christian? Ask others this question and conduct a survey of your group. *Write down* your views.

Assignment No.
Time allowed

44: The plot against Jesus

Objective

To be aware of the circumstances of Jesus' arrest and eventual death.

1 *Opinion*:

After reading the passage, answer the following:

(a) Why do you think the people might have rioted if Jesus was arrested during the day? *Discuss* this and *write down* your ideas in your folder.

(b) How would you describe the chief priests and teachers of the Law? *Write down* your ideas.

(c) Do you think Jesus knew he was going to be arrested eventually? *Write down* your ideas and give reasons for your views.

(d) If Jesus had not been arrested and prevented from teaching his followers, do you think he would have had other messages for them?

2 *Research*:

Find out as much as you can about the festival of the Passover. Study the index of textbooks and from them *write down* a brief summary of what the Passover is. Why is it an important event for Jews all over the world today?

Assignment No.	
Time allowed	

45: Jesus is anointed at Bethany

Objectives

To be aware of the importance attached to Jesus' anointing at Bethany.

To consider Jesus' purpose on earth.

1 Find out the meaning of these words from the story (use a dictionary if necessary):

anoint, alabaster.

2 Make a *brief summary* of the story, saying where the event took place and why some people were angry.

3 *Find out*:
   (a) What name is given to the skin disease that Simon probably had?
   (b) What evidence shows that Jesus knew he would soon die? Refer to the text in your answer.
   (c) What do these words of Jesus mean? Write a brief statement.

   You will always have the poor with you, and any time you want to, you can help them. But you will not always have me. . . .

4 *Opinion*:
   (a) The story mentions that some of the people were angry. If they had understood Jesus' purpose on earth, would they still have been angry? Why?
   (b) Do you think church buildings and property should be sold to help with the housing shortage, or the poor in the Third World; should *all* church property, *some* church property or *no* church property be sold to help the poor? *Discuss* this with others and *make a list* of points for and against.

5 *Research*:
   How might the actions of the woman show that she knew Jesus to be the Messiah?

   Look up the word *anointing* in a textbook to help you answer the question.

Assignment No.

Time allowed

46: Judas agrees to betray Jesus

Objectives

To examine some reasons why Judas may have betrayed Jesus.

To understand what betrayal means.

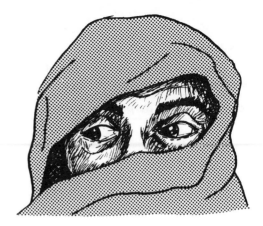

1 Read the story. What does the word *betray* mean? (Use a dictionary, if necessary.)

2 *Complete the following sentences*:
  (*a*) Jesus was betrayed by . . . .
  (*b*) . . . . went to the chief . . . . in order to betray . . . .
  (*c*) If someone is called a Judas they are said to be . . . .

3 *Opinion*:
  (*a*) Give as many reasons as you can why you think the disciple that Jesus shared part of his life with decided to betray him. You may wish to use a textbook or discuss this with others.
  (*b*) Some people think that Judas belonged to the Zealot party and hoped that Jesus was going to lead a revolution against the Romans. What do you think about this?
  (*c*) What reasons might someone have to betray a friend or neighbour? What reasons do people have for betraying their beliefs, or their country?

LIFE AND TEACHING OF JESUS

V · Jesus' last week on Earth

| Assignment No. |
| Time allowed |

47: Jesus eats the Passover meal with his disciples

Objectives

To learn of the preparations made by the disciples for the Passover meal.

To show the plot against Jesus unfolding as time runs out for him.

1 After reading the account from Mark's Gospel, *complete these sentences:*
   (a) . . . . were killed for the Passover meal.
   (b) A man carrying a . . . . will meet you.
   (c) The "teacher" in the story is . . . .
   (d) The house with the upstairs room is in the city of . . . .

2 *Find out:*
   (a) What three things were mentioned about the upstairs room?
   (b) What was the sign or signal the disciples had to look out for?
   (c) In whose house was the upstairs room? Try to find out by looking at some books that mention this story.
   (d) What event in Jewish history does the Passover festival celebrations remember? Say why the Passover is still an important festival for Jews today. See the book of Exodus, chapter 12, if you need help.

3 *Research:*
   (a) Make two columns, like the ones below, with the headings and symbols filled in. Find from a textbook what each of these symbols used in the Passover meal represents and write it in on your chart.

Symbols	*Represent*
Matzoth	
An egg	
Roasted lamb bone	
Bitter herbs	
Salt water	
Parsley	
Haroset	
Four cups of wine	

   (b) Find out the meaning of the word *atonement* in the Jewish faith.

48 : The Last Supper (1)

Objectives

To learn what happened and what was said at the Last Supper.

To show that Jesus knew he would be betrayed.

1 After reading the story, write a *short summary* explaining where Jesus and his disciples were, what Jesus said to them, and why the disciples were upset.

2 *Complete the following sentences*:
   (a) I tell you that . . . .
   (b) It will be one of . . . .
   (c) The Son of . . . .
   (d) It would have been better . . . .

3 *Find out*:
   (a) In what other story did Jesus feed people?
   (b) Who is the Son of Man? List other titles that were given to this person.
   (c) What food do you think the disciples might have been eating?

4 *Research*:
   (a) Jesus said: "The Son of Man will die as the scriptures say . . ." What does the Old Testament book of Isaiah (chapter 53) say about this? Look in the book of Isaiah and make a brief note.
   (b) Find out from the Gospels and from pictures and other sources the names of all those who were probably present at the Last Supper. *Make a list.*

LIFE AND TEACHING OF JESUS   **V · Jesus' last week on Earth**

Assignment No.
Time allowed

49: The Last Supper (2)

Objectives

To know the words spoken by Jesus to his followers at the Last Supper and appreciate the importance attached to them today.

To learn why Christians specially remember this supper.

To come to an understanding of what the bread and the wine represent and its importance for Christians.

1 Read the account from Mark's Gospel, write down the words spoken by Jesus when he:
  (a) took the bread,
  (b) took the cup.

2 *Find out*:
  (a) What do these words mean? Find or make up a definition for each word:
    sacrament, covenant, testament, communion, eucharist, mass.
  (b) What do the bread and the wine represent?
  (c) What is the church service which includes the bread and the wine called? (Find three names.)
  (d) Holy Communion is a sacrament. Find out if Christians have any other sacraments and say what they are.

3 *Research*:
  (a) Ask people who go to church and who go to communion regularly:
    (i) Why do they go?
    (ii) What does the occasion mean for them?
  (b) Read all the Bible accounts of this occasion, and see if you can find out why this service is thought of as a thanksgiving as well as a memorial.
  (c) Look at the service book of a Christian church and find this service. See what words in the service have come straight from the Bible story.

50: Jesus predicts Peter's denial

Objectives

To show that Jesus can predict what others will say and do.

To think about the value of friendship.

To learn about martyrs (people who have died for their faith).

1 After reading the story, *make three columns* headed as below. *Write in* the words spoken by: *(a)* Jesus, *(b)* Peter, *(c)* The disciples.

Words spoken by Jesus	*Words of Peter*	*Words of the disciples*

2 *Find out*:
  (a) Who is the shepherd in this story?
  (b) Who are the sheep in this story?
  (c) To which region did Jesus say he would go after he was raised from the dead? Name *three* towns in this region.
  (d) Which Old Testament scripture was Jesus referring to?

3 *Opinion*:
  (a) How do you think Peter felt when Jesus told him he would deny him? Write down your views.
  (b) True friendship means never turning your back or forgetting a friend in need. Do you agree with this statement? *Write down* your views.
  (c) Is the friendship and loyalty of others important for you?
  (d) Does friendship mean complete loyalty at all times? Is there a problem for those who might say *yes* to this question?

4 *Research*:
  Find out about people who have had to die for their faith in the past, or who are suffering for their faith at the present time. *Write a paragraph* about them.

LIFE AND TEACHING OF JESUS   **V · Jesus' last week on Earth**

Assignment No.

Time allowed

51 : Jesus prays in Gethsemane

Objectives

To show Jesus' humanity.

To examine Jesus' relationship with God.

1 After reading the story, *find out the meanings* of the following words (use a dictionary if necessary):

(a) distress (b) anguish (c) temptation

2 *Match up the beginnings and endings of the sentences*:

Beginnings	Endings
(a) They came to a place . . .	. . . is now being handed over to the power of sinful men.
(b) Jesus said, "Sit here . . .	. . . sorrow in my heart is so great that it almost crushes me."
(c) Jesus said to Peter, James and John, "The . . .	. . . of suffering from me.
(d) Jesus prayed that, if possible . . .	. . . disciples asleep.
(e) "Father, all things . . .	. . . called Gethsemane.
(f) Take this cup . . .	. . . pray that you will not fall into temptation.
(g) Yet not what I . . .	. . . has come.
(h) When Jesus returned he found his . . .	. . . while I pray."
(i) Jesus said, "Weren't you able . . .	. . . are possible for you.
(j) Keep watch and . . .	. . . willing, but the flesh is weak.
(k) The spirit is . . .	. . . he might not have to go through that time of suffering.
(l) The hour . . .	. . . want, but what you want."
(m) The Son of Man . . .	. . . to stay awake even for one hour?"

3 *Find out*:

(a) What happened for Jesus to say ". . . the spirit is willing but the flesh is weak"?

(b) Who was Jesus referring to as "the man who is betraying me"?

(c) What is the meaning of the expression used by Jesus, ". . . take this cup of suffering away from me"?

4 *Opinion*:

(a) How does this story show the human side of Jesus?

(b) What does "The hour has come" mean?

(c) How would you describe Jesus' state of mind at the beginning of the passage (verses 32–35)?

LIFE AND TEACHING OF JESUS   **V · Jesus' last week on Earth**

Text © Andrew Lawrence 1990. Illustration © Richard Smith 1990

| Assignment No. |
| Time allowed |

52: The Trial before the High Priest

Objectives

To learn what happened to Jesus before the Jewish Council – the Sanhedrin.

To note the character of some of the Jews and the unfairness of Jesus' trial.

1 Make *four columns* with headings, as below. Read the *three* accounts of Jesus' trial carefully. Using these accounts find the answers to complete each box.

Questions about the trial	Matthew	Mark	Luke
Where was Jesus taken after his arrest?	High Priest's house	High Priest's house	Before the Council

Write these questions in the left-hand column:

Who was present?
What time of day was it when Jesus was taken?
What were those present trying to do to Jesus?
How did the witnesses behave?
What was Jesus accused of?

What was said about the temple?
What did Jesus reply to the lies?
What did Jesus reply to the question, "Are you the Messiah?"?
How was Jesus mocked?

2 *Find out:*

(a) Why was Jesus' answer to the question put to him by the High Priest considered blasphemous?

Check again the meaning of *blasphemy* from the task sheet – "Jesus heals the man with a paralysed hand".

(b) Why did the High Priest tear his robes?

3 *Opinion:*

Is the fact that Jesus remained almost silent important? *Write down* your ideas.

4 *Research:*

Was Jesus' trial and sentence legal under Jewish Law?

You will need to look in a textbook or ask your teacher about the rules for conducting a trial and passing sentence. Look at the *three* accounts to see if the rules you have discovered may have been broken in any way. *Make a list* of your findings.

LIFE AND TEACHING OF JESUS

V · Jesus' last week on Earth

Assignment No.

Time allowed

53 : Peter's denial

Objectives

To discover why Peter denied knowing Jesus.

To think about the position Peter found himself in and whether he deserves some sympathy.

To learn more about Simon Peter and his life.

1 After reading the passage from Mark's Gospel, *complete these sentences:*
 (a) .... first said to Peter that he had been with Jesus.
 (b) Peter denied he had been with Jesus .... times.
 (c) When he was accused Peter said, ...
 (d) Peter was from the region of ....
 (e) Peter cried because ....

2 *Find out*:
 Why did Peter deny he had been with Jesus?

3 *Opinion*:
 (a) How do you think Peter must have been feeling:
   (i) When he was questioned?
   (ii) After the cock had finished crowing?
 (b) Can a person be a secret disciple or a silent witness? Think what the expressions mean first. *Write down* your views.

4 *Research*:
 Find out as much as you can, using a textbook, encyclopaedia, or the Gospels and the Acts of the Apostles, about the life of Peter, before the death of Jesus and afterwards, and *draw up a flow chart* of his life.

LIFE AND TEACHING OF JESUS   **V · Jesus' last week on Earth**

| Assignment No. |
| Time allowed |

54: Jesus is brought before Pilate

Objectives

To be aware of Mark and Luke's accounts of Jesus' trial.

To examine where the Gospel writers place the blame for Jesus' death.

To appreciate the differences in the two accounts.

1 *Tasks*:

Read the two accounts of Jesus' trial before Pilate.

Imagine you are a detective trying to piece together what really happened to Jesus when he was before Pilate. *Answer the questions* by putting the information *in the correct column*.

Questions	Mark	Luke
When was the trial held?		
Who was there?		
What did they accuse Jesus of?		
What did they do to Jesus?		
What did Pilate say to Jesus?		
What was Jesus' reaction to the questions put to him?		

2 Using the information you have put into the three columns, *write a brief summary* of Jesus' trial before Pilate.

3 *Find out*:

Why was the charge of blasphemy before the High Priest's Council changed by the chief priests and elders, to "misleading the people" and "starting a riot"?

4 *Research*:

Find out about the law against blasphemy today. Which religion does it protect? Do you think there should be a law to protect people's religious feelings, and if so, should it protect all religions? Get views and *write down* the case on one side or the other.

LIFE AND TEACHING OF JESUS V · **Jesus' last week on Earth**

<table>
<tr><td>Assignment No.</td></tr>
<tr><td>Time allowed</td></tr>
</table>

55 : Jesus is sentenced to death

Objectives

To learn of Jesus and Barabbas' trial before Pilate.

To examine who is to blame for Jesus' death.

1 After reading the passage, *write a summary of the story* and include the following:
(a) Where the trial took place.
(b) The custom observed by Pilate.
(c) The reason why the chief priests handed Jesus over to Pilate.
(d) The reason why many wanted Barabbas set free.
(e) The words shouted by the crowd.

2 *Find out*:
(a) Why was Barabbas put in prison?
(b) Who stirred up the crowd to ask for Barabbas' release?
(c) What evidence suggests that Pilate thought Jesus was not an ordinary man?
(d) Try to find out what the word *Bar* means (the prefix to *Abbas* in *Barabbas*).
(e) Barabbas was a *Zealot*. Try to find information about the Zealot movement; when the movement began, what the movement set out to achieve, the actions of the group, and the beliefs of its members.

3 *Opinion*:
(a) Think carefully about the story and write a character profile of Pilate. For example, was he a thoughtful man, did he make his own decisions, did he believe in fair play?
(b) Who do you think should take the blame for Jesus' death?

4 *Research*:
Find out the meaning of the word 'anti-Semitism'. An excuse for anti-Semitism has often been the idea that the Jews killed Jesus. From your study of the Gospels, is this true? If it was true, would it justify killing Jews today? What do you think Jesus would have answered to these questions? *Write a short report* on this subject.

Assignment No.

Time allowed

56: The soldiers mock Jesus

Objectives

To learn of the humiliation and torment experienced by Jesus at the hands of the Roman soldiers.

To think about whether Jesus' suffering can help others in times of crisis.

1 Read the story and *complete these sentences*:
   (a) Jesus was taken by . . . . to the courtyard of . . . .
   (b) They dressed Jesus in . . . . and made . . . . from thorn . . . . and put it on . . . .
   (c) The soldiers shouted . . . .
   (d) They . . . . over the head with . . . . and . . . . on him.
   (e) After the soldiers finished they took the . . . . and put his own . . . .
   (f) The soldiers led Jesus out to . . . .

2 *Find out*:
   What cruelties were inflicted on Jesus?

3 *Opinion*:
   Why do you think the soldiers treated Jesus in the way they did?

4 *Research*:
   Either write a *short article* about bullying at school, or about violence against women or children by people stronger than them;

   or find out what happens to prisoners in countries where police and prison officers feel free to do what they like to them; you may want to write to Amnesty International and take up the cause of a political prisoner somewhere in the world today.

57 : The Crucifixion

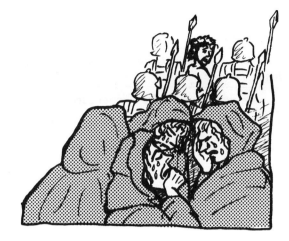

Objectives

To learn of the differences in the accounts of the crucifixion.

To answer the question: did Jesus have to die?

1 Read the *three* passages and *complete these sentences*:

(a) . . . . carried Jesus' cross.

(b) Jesus said to the women of Jerusalem, ...

(c) The name of the place where Jesus was crucified is called . . . .

(d) Jesus said to those responsible for crucifying him, ...

(e) The time of day when Jesus was crucified was . . . .

(f) . . . . was written and placed on the cross above Jesus' head.

(g) . . . . was given to Jesus when he was on the cross.

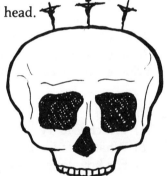

2 *Find out*:

(a) What is the most important symbol for Christians?

(b) On what day of the year do Christians especially remember the crucifixion?

(c) What does the word *Golgotha* mean?

3 *Opinion*:

What evidence is there in Luke's Gospel to suggest that wrongdoers can be forgiven?

4 *Research*:

(a) Ask as many people as you can how they think a Christian would respond to the following statement:

'If Jesus was really the Son of God, he would not have allowed himself to die.'

Write a *short summary* of their views.

or

(b) Find out the main arguments for and against capital punishment. *Write a paragraph* on the subject saying what you think about it and why. Does the crucifixion of Jesus affect your view on this subject?

LIFE AND TEACHING OF JESUS

V · Jesus' last week on Earth

58: The Death of Jesus

Objectives

To learn of the events surrounding the death of Jesus.

To note variations in the Gospel accounts.

To find out the last words Jesus said before he died.

1 After reading the three accounts, *make four columns* and head them *Questions, Matthew, Mark* and *Luke*. Write these questions in the questions column and answer them in the other columns:

What time did darkness fall?
How long was it dark?
What did Jesus say at three o'clock?
What drink was offered to Jesus?
At what time did Jesus die?
What was said by the soldier?
What were the names of the women present?
What events occurred as Jesus died?

2 *Find out*:
   (a) Which Old Testament prophet did some people present think Jesus was calling to?
   (b) What does *Eli, Eli, lema sabachthani* mean?
   (c) For how long was Jesus slowly dying on the cross? To answer this you will need to look back at the last task sheet, "The Crucifixion", from Mark's Gospel, to see what time it was when Jesus was crucified.
   (d) How old was Jesus approximately when he died?
   (e) Use a textbook to find out the meaning of the tearing of the Temple curtain.
   (f) According to Luke's Gospel, what did some people do as they left the place of the crucifixion to go home?

3 *Research*:
The Gospels mention that many women followed Jesus. Ask other people why they think very little is mentioned of them. *Write up* a summary of their views.

Assignment No.

Time allowed

59: The Burial of Jesus

Objectives

To learn of the burial of Jesus from three Gospels.

To know who were involved in the burial.

To consider whether Jesus returned to life and walked out of the tomb

1 Read the *three* accounts carefully and then write a brief, though accurate, message saying who buried Jesus, where the body was laid to rest and when this happened.

2 *Complete these sentences*:
   (a) . . . . asked for the body of Jesus. He was from . . . .
   (b) The tomb Jesus was placed in had been dug from . . . .
   (c) The women who went to see the body were . . . .
   (d) When the women arrived home they . . . .
   (e) The man who asked for the body had been waiting for . . . .

3 *Find out*:
   (a) What evidence from Luke's Gospel suggests that not all the members of the Sanhedrin (Jewish Council) were against Jesus?
   (b) What evidence suggests that Pilate had not attended the crucifixion?

4 *Opinion*:
   Do you think Joseph was brave, stupid or clever, when he asked if he could have the body of Jesus? *Write down* your views along with your reasons.

5 *Research*:
   Study the Gospel stories very carefully from the time Jesus' body was removed from the cross until the women found the empty tomb. Is it possible that Jesus recovered, rolled the stone away from inside, and walked out? Or could there be any other explanation? Treat the case as a detective would; ask others also, and note all the arguments for the different theories.

60 : The Resurrection

Objectives

To learn of the variations in the resurrection accounts.

To consider how Jesus rose from the dead: physically or spiritually.

To find out if the resurrection is important for Christians today.

1 Read the three accounts and *make four columns* headed *Questions, Matthew, Mark* and *Luke*, and copy the questions below into the questions column; write the answers in the appropriate column:

Which women went to the tomb?
When did the women go to the tomb?
What were the women carrying?
What did the women say as they walked?
What happened to the ground as the women approached the tomb?
How many angels are referred to?
What did they say?

In which places were the angels seen?
What was the reaction of the guards?
What did the women do on leaving the tomb?
What did the women tell the disciples they had seen?
How did the disciples react?

2 *Find out*:
   (a) What evidence is there, in the walk to Emmaus, to support the view that Jesus knew he would suffer?
   (b) Is there evidence to support the view that Cleopas may have known Peter?
   (c) When did Cleopas recognize Jesus?
   (d) How did Cleopas and his friend describe the experience with Jesus?
   (e) What did the two men say to the disciples?
   (f) What does the word *apostle* mean?
   (g) Who were the apostles? (Try to find 11, 12 or 13 names.)

3 *Opinion*:
   (a) Why do you think the disciples did not believe the women when they reported Jesus was not to be found in the tomb? *Write down* your views.
   (b) Do you think Jesus rose from the dead in bodily form? Some Christians doubt this happened. What are your views?

4 *Research*:
   How important is the resurrection of Jesus for his followers today? Make *three* columns like the ones below and ask *twenty* Christians for their opinions. *Tick a box and write the reason.*

Very important	Important	Not important	Reason

LIFE AND TEACHING OF JESUS

V · Jesus' last week on Earth

Assignment No.

Time allowed

61 : The Ascension

Objectives

To learn the parting instructions of Jesus to his disciples.

To note the differences in the recordings.

To think about whether Jesus rose from earth physically.

1 *Make a summary of the stories* and mention what Jesus said, what the disciples did, and the thoughts of some of them.

2 What does the word *ascension* mean? (Use a dictionary if you need to.)

3 *Find out:*
   (a) Which place was Jesus at when he was taken to heaven?
   (b) What was Jesus doing as he was taken away?

4 *Opinion:*
   (a) Why do you think the disciples were joyous that Jesus had been taken away from them? *Write down* your views.
   (b) Why might a Christian mention this story to justify knocking on people's doors to talk about their faith to others?

5 *Research:*
   The words Jesus spoke have inspired Christians to tell others about him and spread their faith; this is called mission. *Either* find out about the missionaries who brought Christianity to Britain and write a paragraph about one of them; *or* find out what other faiths believe about converting people to their beliefs.

1 : Matthew's account of the birth of Jesus

Matthew 1.18–25

18This was how the birth of Jesus Christ took place. His mother Mary was engaged to Joseph, but before they were married, she found out that she was going to have a baby by the Holy Spirit. 19Joseph was a man who always did what was right, but he did not want to disgrace Mary publicly; so he made plans to break the engagement privately. 20While he was thinking about this, an angel of the Lord appeared to him in a dream and said, "Joseph, descendant of David, do not be afraid to take Mary to be your wife. For it is by the Holy Spirit that she has conceived. 21She will have a son, and you will name him Jesus—because he will save his people from their sins."

22Now all this happened in order to make what the Lord had said through the prophet come true. 23"A virgin will become pregnant and have a son, and he will be called Immanuel" (which means, "God is with us").

24So when Joseph woke up, he married Mary, as the angel of the Lord had told him to do. 25But he had no sexual relations with her before she gave birth to her son. And Joseph named him Jesus.

Matthew 2.1–12

VISITORS FROM THE EAST

1Jesus was born in the town of Bethlehem in Judaea, during the time when Herod was king. Soon afterwards, some men who studied the stars came from the east to Jerusalem 2and asked, "Where is the baby born to be the king of the Jews? We saw his star when it came up in the east, and we have come to worship him."

3When King Herod heard about this, he was very upset, and so was everyone else in Jerusalem. 4He called together all the chief priests and the teachers of the Law and asked them, "Where will the Messiah be born?"

5"In the town of Bethlehem in Judaea," they answered. "For this is what the prophet wrote:

6'Bethlehem in the land of Judah,
    you are by no means the least of the leading cities of Judah;
for from you will come a leader
    who will guide my people Israel.'"

7So Herod called the visitors from the east to a secret meeting and found out from them the exact time the star had appeared. 8Then he sent them to Bethlehem with these instructions: "Go and make a careful search for the child, and when you find him, let me know, so that I too may go and worship him."

9-10And so they left, and on their way they saw the same star they had seen in the east. When they saw it, how happy they were, what joy was theirs! It went ahead of them until it stopped over the place where the child was. 11They went into the house, and when they saw the child with his mother Mary, they knelt down and worshipped him. They brought out their gifts of gold, frankincense, and myrrh, and presented them to him.

12Then they returned to their country by another road, since God had warned them in a dream not to go back to Herod.

2 : Luke's account of the birth of Jesus

Luke 2.1–7

1At that time the Emperor Augustus ordered a census to be taken throughout the Roman Empire. 2When this first census took place, Quirinius was the governor of Syria. 3Everyone, then, went to register himself, each to his own town.

4Joseph went from the town of Nazareth in Galilee to the town of Bethlehem in Judaea, the birthplace of King David. Joseph went there because he was a descendant of David. 5He went to register with Mary, who was promised in marriage to him. She was pregnant, 6and while they were in Bethlehem, the time came for her to have her baby. 7She gave birth to her first son, wrapped him in strips of cloth and laid him in a manger—there was no room for them to stay in the inn.

Luke 2.8–20

THE SHEPHERDS AND THE ANGELS

8There were some shepherds in that part of the country who were spending the night in the fields, taking care of their flocks. 9An angel of the Lord appeared to them, and the glory of the Lord shone over them. They were terribly afraid, 10but the angel said to them, "Don't be afraid! I am here with good news for you, which will bring great joy to all the people. 11This very day in David's town your Saviour was born—Christ the Lord! 12And this is what will prove it to you: you will find a baby wrapped in strips of cloth and lying in a manger."

13Suddenly a great army of heaven's angels appeared with the angel, singing praises to God:

14"Glory to God in the highest heaven,
    and peace on earth to those with whom he is pleased!"

15When the angels went away from them back into heaven, the shepherds said to one another, "Let's go to Bethlehem and see this thing that has happened, which the Lord has told us."

16So they hurried off and found Mary and Joseph and saw the baby lying in the manger. 17When the shepherds saw him, they told them what the angel had said about the child. 18All who heard it were amazed at what the shepherds said. 19Mary remembered all these things and thought deeply about them. 20The shepherds went back, singing praises to God for all they had heard and seen; it had been just as the angel had told them.

3: The baptism of Jesus

Matthew 3.13–17

¹³At that time Jesus arrived from Galilee and came to John at the Jordan to be baptized by him. ¹⁴But John tried to make him change his mind. "I ought to be baptized by you," John said, "and yet you have come to me!"

¹⁵But Jesus answered him, "Let it be so for now. For in this way we shall do all that God requires." So John agreed.

¹⁶As soon as Jesus was baptized, he came up out of the water. Then heaven was opened to him, and he saw the Spirit of God coming down like a dove and alighting on him. ¹⁷Then a voice said from heaven, "This is my own dear Son, with whom I am pleased."

4: The temptation of Jesus

Luke 4.1–13

¹Jesus returned from the Jordan full of the Holy Spirit and was led by the Spirit into the desert, ²where he was tempted by the Devil for forty days. In all that time he ate nothing, so that he was hungry when it was over.

³The Devil said to him, "If you are God's Son, order this stone to turn into bread."

⁴But Jesus answered, "The scripture says, 'Man cannot live on bread alone.'"

⁵Then the Devil took him up and showed him in a second all the kingdoms of the world. ⁶"I will give you all this power and all this wealth," the Devil told him. "It has all been handed over to me, and I can give it to anyone I choose. ⁷All this will be yours, then, if you worship me."

⁸Jesus answered, "The scripture says, 'Worship the Lord your God and serve only him!'"

⁹Then the Devil took him to Jerusalem and set him on the highest point of the Temple, and said to him, "If you are God's Son, throw yourself down from here. ¹⁰For the scripture says, 'God will order his angels to take good care of you.' ¹¹It also says, 'They will hold you up with their hands so that not even your feet will be hurt on the stones.'"

¹²But Jesus answered, "The scripture says, 'Do not put the Lord your God to the test.'"

¹³When the Devil finished tempting Jesus in every way, he left him for a while.

Matthew 4.1–11

¹Then the Spirit led Jesus into the desert to be tempted by the Devil. ²After spending forty days and nights without food, Jesus was hungry. ³Then the Devil came to him and said, "If you are God's Son, order these stones to turn into bread."

⁴But Jesus answered, "The scripture says, 'Man cannot live on bread alone, but needs every word that God speaks.'"

⁵Then the Devil took Jesus to Jerusalem, the Holy City, set him on the highest point of the Temple, ⁶and said to him, "If you are God's Son, throw yourself down, for the scripture says,

'God will give orders to his angels about you;
  they will hold you up with their hands,
    so that not even your feet will be hurt on the stones.'"

⁷Jesus answered, "But the scripture also says, 'Do not put the Lord your God to the test.'"

⁸Then the Devil took Jesus to a very high mountain and showed him all the kingdoms of the world in all their greatness. ⁹"All this I will give you," the Devil said, "if you kneel down and worship me."

¹⁰Then Jesus answered, "Go away, Satan! The scripture says, 'Worship the Lord your God and serve only him!'"

¹¹Then the Devil left Jesus; and angels came and helped him.

5: Jesus calls four fishermen to be followers

Mark 1.14–20

¹⁴Jesus went to Galilee and preached the Good News from God. ¹⁵"The right time has come," he said, "and the Kingdom of God is near! Turn away from your sins and believe the Good News!"

¹⁶As Jesus walked along the shore of Lake Galilee, he saw two fishermen, Simon and his brother Andrew, catching fish with a net. ¹⁷Jesus said to them, "Come with me, and I will teach you to catch men." ¹⁸At once

they left their nets and went with him.

¹⁹He went a little farther on and saw two other brothers, James and John, the sons of Zebedee. They were in their boat getting their nets ready. ²⁰As soon as Jesus saw them, he called them; they left their father Zebedee in the boat with the hired men and went with Jesus.

6 : Jesus calls Levi

Mark 2.13–17

[13]Jesus went back again to the shore of Lake Galilee. A crowd came to him, and he started teaching them. [14]As he walked along, he saw a tax collector, Levi son of Alphaeus, sitting in his office. Jesus said to him, "Follow me." Levi got up and followed him.

[15]Later on Jesus was having a meal in Levi's house. A large number of tax collectors and other outcasts were following Jesus, and many of them joined him and his disciples at the table. [16]Some teachers of the Law, who were Pharisees, saw that Jesus was eating with these outcasts and tax collectors, so they asked his disciples, "Why does he eat with such people?"

[17]Jesus heard them and answered, "People who are well do not need a doctor, but only those who are sick. I have not come to call respectable people, but outcasts."

7 : Jesus heals a paralysed man

Mark 2.1–12

[1]A few days later Jesus went back to Capernaum, and the news spread that he was at home. [2]So many people came together that there was no room left, not even out in front of the door. Jesus was preaching the message to them [3]when four men arrived, carrying a paralysed man to Jesus. [4]Because of the crowd, however, they could not get the man to him. So they made a hole in the roof right above the place where Jesus was. When they had made an opening, they let the man down, lying on his mat. [5]Seeing how much faith they had, Jesus said to the paralysed man, "My son, your sins are forgiven."

[6]Some teachers of the Law who were sitting there thought to themselves, [7]"How does he dare to talk like this? This is blasphemy! God is the only one who can forgive sins!"

[8]At once Jesus knew what they were thinking, so he said to them, "Why do you think such things? [9]Is it easier to say to this paralysed man, 'Your sins are forgiven', or to say, 'Get up, pick up your mat, and walk'? [10]I will prove to you, then, that the Son of Man has authority on earth to forgive sins." So he said to the paralysed man, [11]"I tell you, get up, pick up your mat, and go home!"

[12]While they all watched, the man got up, picked up his mat, and hurried away. They were all completely amazed and praised God, saying, "We have never seen anything like this!"

8 : The question about fasting

Mark 2.18–22

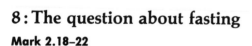

[18]On one occasion the followers of John the Baptist and the Pharisees were fasting. Some people came to Jesus and asked him, "Why is it that the disciples of John the Baptist and the disciples of the Pharisees fast, but yours do not?"

[19]Jesus answered, "Do you expect the guests at a wedding party to go without food? Of course not! As long as the bridegroom is with them, they will not do that. [20]But the day will come when the bridegroom will be taken away from them, and then they will fast.

[21]"No one uses a piece of new cloth to patch up an old coat, because the new patch will shrink and tear off some of the old cloth, making an even bigger hole. [22]Nor does anyone pour new wine into used wineskins, because the wine will burst the skins, and both the wine and the skins will be ruined. Instead, new wine must be poured into fresh wineskins."

9 : The question about the Sabbath

Mark 2.23–28

²³Jesus was walking through some cornfields on the Sabbath. As his disciples walked along with him, they began to pick the ears of corn. ²⁴So the Pharisees said to Jesus, "Look, it is against our Law for your disciples to do that on the Sabbath!"

²⁵Jesus answered, "Have you never read what David did that time when he needed something to eat? He and his men were hungry, ²⁶so he went into the house of God and ate the bread offered to God. This happened when Abiathar was the High Priest. According to our Law only the priests may eat this bread—but David ate it and even gave it to his men."

²⁷And Jesus concluded, "The Sabbath was made for the good of man; man was not made for the Sabbath. ²⁸So the Son of Man is Lord even of the Sabbath."

10 : Jesus heals the man with a paralysed hand

Mark 3.1–6

¹Then Jesus went back to the synagogue, where there was a man who had a paralysed hand. ²Some people were there who wanted to accuse Jesus of doing wrong; so they watched him closely to see whether he would heal the man on the Sabbath. ³Jesus said to the man, "Come up here to the front." ⁴Then he asked the people, "What does our Law allow us to do on the Sabbath? To help or to harm? To save a man's life or to destroy it?"

But they did not say a thing. ⁵Jesus was angry as he looked round at them, but at the same time he felt sorry for them, because they were so stubborn and wrong. Then he said to the man, "Stretch out your hand." He stretched it out, and it became well again. ⁶So the Pharisees left the synagogue and met at once with some members of Herod's party, and they made plans to kill Jesus.

11 : Peter's declaration at Caesarea Philippi

Matthew 16.13–20

¹³Jesus went to the territory near the town of Caesarea Philippi, where he asked his disciples, "Who do people say the Son of Man is?"

¹⁴"Some say John the Baptist," they answered. "Others say Elijah, while others say Jeremiah or some other prophet."

¹⁵"What about you?" he asked them. "Who do you say I am?"

¹⁶Simon Peter answered, "You are the Messiah, the Son of the living God."

¹⁷"Good for you, Simon son of John!" answered Jesus. "For this truth did not come to you from any human being, but it was given to you directly by my Father in heaven. ¹⁸And so I tell you, Peter: you are a rock, and on this rock foundation I will build my church, and not even death will ever be able to overcome it. ¹⁹I will give you the keys of the Kingdom of heaven; what you prohibit on earth will be prohibited in heaven, and what you permit on earth will be permitted in heaven."

²⁰Then Jesus ordered his disciples not to tell anyone that he was the Messiah.

12 : The Transfiguration of Jesus

Mark 9.2–9

²Six days later Jesus took with him Peter, James, and John, and led them up a high mountain, where they were alone. As they looked on, a change came over Jesus, ³and his clothes became shining white—whiter than anyone in the world could wash them. ⁴Then the three disciples saw Elijah and Moses talking with Jesus. ⁵Peter spoke up and said to Jesus, "Teacher, how good it is that we are here! We will make three tents, one for you, one for Moses, and one for Elijah." ⁶He and the others were so frightened that he did not know what to say.

⁷Then a cloud appeared and covered them with its shadow, and a voice came from the cloud, "This is my own dear Son—listen to him!" ⁸They took a quick look round but did not see anyone else; only Jesus was with them.

⁹As they came down the mountain, Jesus ordered them, "Don't tell anyone what you have seen, until the Son of Man has risen from death."

13 : Jesus at the home of Simon the Pharisee

Luke 7.36–50

³⁶A Pharisee invited Jesus to have dinner with him, and Jesus went to his house and sat down to eat. ³⁷In that town was a woman who lived a sinful life. She heard that Jesus was eating in the Pharisee's house, so she brought an alabaster jar full of perfume ³⁸and stood behind Jesus, by his feet, crying and wetting his feet with her tears. Then she dried his feet with her hair, kissed them, and poured the perfume on them. ³⁹When the Pharisee saw this, he said to himself, "If this man really were a prophet, he would know who this woman is who is touching him; he would know what kind of sinful life she lives!"

⁴⁰Jesus spoke up and said to him, "Simon, I have something to tell you."

"Yes, Teacher," he said, "tell me."

⁴¹"There were two men who owed money to a money-lender," Jesus began. "One owed him five hundred silver coins, and the other owed him fifty. ⁴²Neither of them could pay him back, so he cancelled the debts of both. Which one, then, will love him more?"

⁴³"I suppose," answered Simon, "that it would be the one who was forgiven more."

"You are right," said Jesus. ⁴⁴Then he turned to the woman and said to Simon, "Do you see this woman? I came into your home, and you gave me no water for my feet, but she has washed my feet with her tears and dried them with her hair. ⁴⁵You did not welcome me with a kiss, but she has not stopped kissing my feet since I came. ⁴⁶You provided no olive-oil for my head, but she has covered my feet with perfume. ⁴⁷I tell you, then, the great love she has shown proves that her many sins have been forgiven. But whoever has been forgiven little shows only a little love."

⁴⁸Then Jesus said to the woman, "Your sins are forgiven."

⁴⁹The others sitting at the table began to say to themselves, "Who is this, who even forgives sins?"

⁵⁰But Jesus said to the woman, "Your faith has saved you; go in peace."

14 : Jesus visits Mary and Martha

Luke 10.38–42

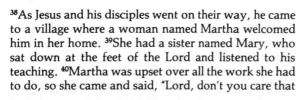

³⁸As Jesus and his disciples went on their way, he came to a village where a woman named Martha welcomed him in her home. ³⁹She had a sister named Mary, who sat down at the feet of the Lord and listened to his teaching. ⁴⁰Martha was upset over all the work she had to do, so she came and said, "Lord, don't you care that

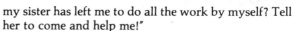

my sister has left me to do all the work by myself? Tell her to come and help me!"

⁴¹The Lord answered her, "Martha, Martha! You are worried and troubled over so many things, ⁴²but just one is needed. Mary has chosen the right thing, and it will not be taken away from her."

15 : Jesus and Zacchaeus

Luke 19.1–10

¹Jesus went on into Jericho and was passing through. ²There was a chief tax collector there named Zacchaeus, who was rich. ³He was trying to see who Jesus was, but he was a little man and could not see Jesus because of the crowd. ⁴So he ran ahead of the crowd and climbed a sycomore tree to see Jesus, who was going to pass that way. ⁵When Jesus came to that place, he looked up and said to Zacchaeus, "Hurry down, Zacchaeus, because I must stay in your house today."

⁶Zacchaeus hurried down and welcomed him with great joy. ⁷All the people who saw it started grumbling. "This man has gone as a guest to the home of a sinner!"

⁸Zacchaeus stood up and said to the Lord, "Listen, sir! I will give half my belongings to the poor, and if I have cheated anyone, I will pay him back four times as much."

⁹Jesus said to him, "Salvation has come to this house today, for this man, also, is a descendant of Abraham. ¹⁰The Son of Man came to seek and to save the lost."

16 : Discipleship

Luke 8.1–3

WOMEN WHO ACCOMPANIED JESUS

¹Some time later Jesus travelled through towns and villages, preaching the Good News about the Kingdom of God. The twelve disciples went with him, ²and so did some women who had been healed of evil spirits and diseases: Mary (who was called Magdalene), from whom seven demons had been driven out; ³Joanna, whose husband Chuza was an officer in Herod's court; and Susanna, and many other women who used their own resources to help Jesus and his disciples.

Luke 9.1–6

JESUS SENDS OUT THE TWELVE DISCIPLES

¹Jesus called the twelve disciples together and gave them power and authority to drive out all demons and to cure diseases. ²Then he sent them out to preach the Kingdom of God and to heal the sick, ³after saying to them, "Take nothing with you for the journey: no stick, no beggar's bag, no food, no money, not even an extra shirt. ⁴Wherever you are welcomed, stay in the same house until you leave that town; ⁵wherever people don't welcome you, leave that town and shake the dust off your feet as a warning to them."

⁶The disciples left and travelled through all the villages, preaching the Good News and healing people everywhere.

Luke 9.51–56

A SAMARITAN VILLAGE REFUSES TO RECEIVE JESUS

⁵¹As the time drew near when Jesus would be taken up to heaven, he made up his mind and set out on his way to Jerusalem. ⁵²He sent messengers ahead of him, who went into a village in Samaria to get everything ready for him. ⁵³But the people there would not receive him, because it was clear that he was on his way to Jerusalem. ⁵⁴When the disciples James and John saw this, they said. "Lord, do you want us to call fire down from heaven to destroy them?"

⁵⁵Jesus turned and rebuked them. ⁵⁶Then Jesus and his disciples went on to another village.

Luke 9.57–62

THE WOULD-BE FOLLOWERS OF JESUS

⁵⁷As they went on their way, a man said to Jesus, "I will follow you wherever you go."

⁵⁸Jesus said to him, "Foxes have holes, and birds have nests, but the Son of Man has nowhere to lie down and rest."

⁵⁹He said to another man, "Follow me."

But that man said, "Sir, first let me go back and bury my father."

⁶⁰Jesus answered, "Let the dead bury their own dead. You go and proclaim the Kingdom of God."

⁶¹Another man said, "I will follow you, sir; but first let me go and say good-bye to my family."

⁶²Jesus said to him, "Anyone who starts to plough and then keeps looking back is of no use to the Kingdom of God."

Luke 10.1–12

JESUS SENDS OUT THE SEVENTY-TWO

¹After this the Lord chose another seventy-two men and sent them out two by two, to go ahead of him to every town and place where he himself was about to go. ²He said to them, "There is a large harvest, but few workers to gather it in. Pray to the owner of the harvest that he will send out workers to gather in his harvest. ³Go! I am sending you like lambs among wolves. ⁴Don't take a purse or a beggar's bag or shoes; don't stop to greet anyone on the road. ⁵Whenever you go into a house, first say, 'Peace be with this house.' ⁶If a peace-loving man lives there, let your greeting of peace remain on him; if not, take back your greeting of peace. ⁷Stay in that same house, eating and drinking whatever they offer you, for a worker should be given his pay. Don't move round from one house to another. ⁸Whenever you go into a town and are made welcome, eat what is set before you, ⁹heal the sick in that town, and say to the people there, 'The Kingdom of God has come near you.' ¹⁰But whenever you go into a town and are not welcomed, go out in the streets and say, ¹¹'Even the dust from your town that sticks to our feet we wipe off against you. But remember that the Kingdom of God has come near you!' ¹²I assure you that on Judgement Day God will show more mercy to Sodom than to that town!

Luke 10.17–20

THE RETURN OF THE SEVENTY-TWO

¹⁷The seventy-two men came back in great joy. "Lord," they said, "even the demons obeyed us when we gave them a command in your name!"

¹⁸Jesus answered them, "I saw Satan fall like lightning from heaven. ¹⁹Listen! I have given you authority, so that you can walk on snakes and scorpions and overcome all the power of the Enemy, and nothing will hurt you. ²⁰But don't be glad because the evil spirits obey you; rather be glad because your names are written in heaven."

LIFE AND TEACHING OF JESUS

VI · Gospel extracts

17 : The Good Samaritan

Luke 10.25–37

²⁵A teacher of the Law came up and tried to trap Jesus. "Teacher," he asked, "what must I do to receive eternal life?"

²⁶Jesus answered him, "What do the Scriptures say? How do you interpret them?"

²⁷The man answered, " 'Love the Lord your God with all your heart, and all your soul, with all your strength, and with all your mind'; and 'Love your neighbour as you love yourself.' "

²⁸"You are right," Jesus replied; "do this and you will live."

²⁹But the teacher of the Law wanted to justify himself, so he asked Jesus, "Who is my neighbour?"

³⁰Jesus answered, "There was once a man who was going down from Jerusalem to Jericho when robbers attacked him, stripped him, and beat him up, leaving him half dead. ³¹It so happened that a priest was going down that road; but when he saw the man, he walked on by, on the other side. ³²In the same way a Levite also came along, went over and looked at the man, and then walked on by, on the other side. ³³But a Samaritan who was travelling that way came upon the man, and when he saw him, his heart was filled with pity. ³⁴He went over to him, poured oil and wine on his wounds and bandaged them; then he put the man on his own animal and took him to an inn, where he took care of him. ³⁵The next day he took out two silver coins and gave them to the innkeeper. 'Take care of him,' he told the innkeeper, 'and when I come back this way, I will pay you whatever else you spend on him.' "

³⁶And Jesus concluded, "In your opinion, which one of these three acted like a neighbour towards the man attacked by the robbers?"

³⁷The teacher of the Law answered, "The one who was kind to him."

Jesus replied, "You go, then, and do the same."

18 : The Rich Fool

Luke 12.13–21

¹³A man in the crowd said to Jesus, "Teacher, tell my brother to divide with me the property our father left us."

¹⁴Jesus answered him, "My friend, who gave me the right to judge or to divide the property between you two?" ¹⁵And he went on to say to them all, "Watch out and guard yourselves from every kind of greed; because a person's true life is not made up of the things he owns, no matter how rich he may be."

¹⁶Then Jesus told them this parable: "There was once a rich man who had land which bore good crops. ¹⁷He began to think to himself, 'I haven't anywhere to keep all my crops. What can I do? ¹⁸This is what I will do,' he told himself: 'I will tear down my barns and build bigger ones, where I will store my corn and all my other goods. ¹⁹Then I will say to myself, Lucky man! You have all the good things you need for many years. Take life easy, eat, drink, and enjoy yourself!' ²⁰But God said to him, 'You fool! This very night you will have to give up your life; then who will get all these things you have kept for yourself?' "

²¹And Jesus concluded, "This is how it is with those who pile up riches for themselves but are not rich in God's sight."

19 : The Pharisee and the Tax Collector

Luke 18.9–14

⁹Jesus also told this parable to people who were sure of their own goodness and despised everybody else. ¹⁰"Once there were two men who went up to the Temple to pray: one was a Pharisee, the other a tax collector. ¹¹"The Pharisee stood apart by himself and prayed, 'I thank you, God, that I am not greedy, dishonest, or an adulterer, like everybody else. I thank you that I am not like that tax collector over there. ¹²I fast two days a week, and I give you a tenth of all my income.'

¹³"But the tax collector stood at a distance and would not even raise his face to heaven, but beat on his breast and said, 'God, have pity on me, a sinner!' ¹⁴I tell you," said Jesus, "the tax collector, and not the Pharisee, was in the right with God when he went home. For everyone who makes himself great will be humbled, and everyone who humbles himself will be made great."

LIFE AND TEACHING OF JESUS

20 : The Ten Bridesmaids

Matthew 25.1–13

¹"At that time the Kingdom of heaven will be like this. Once there were ten girls who took their oil lamps and went out to meet the bridegroom. ²Five of them were foolish, and the other five were wise. ³The foolish ones took their lamps but did not take any extra oil with them, ⁴while the wise ones took containers full of oil for their lamps. ⁵The bridegroom was late in coming, so the girls began to nod and fall asleep.

⁶"It was already midnight when the cry rang out, 'Here is the bridegroom! Come and meet him!' ⁷The ten girls woke up and trimmed their lamps. ⁸Then the foolish ones said to the wise ones, 'Let us have some of your oil, because our lamps are going out.' ⁹'No, indeed,' the wise ones answered, 'there is not enough for you and for us. Go to the shop and buy some for yourselves.' ¹⁰So the foolish girls went off to buy some oil; and while they were gone, the bridegroom arrived. The five girls who were ready went in with him to the wedding feast, and the door was closed.

¹¹"Later the other girls arrived. 'Sir, sir! Let us in!' they cried out. ¹²'Certainly not! I don't know you,' the bridegroom answered."

¹³And Jesus concluded, "Be on your guard, then, because you do not know the day or the hour."

21 : The Sower

Matthew 13.1–9

¹That same day Jesus left the house and went to the lake-side, where he sat down to teach. ²The crowd that gathered round him was so large that he got into a boat and sat in it, while the crowd stood on the shore. ³He used parables to tell them many things.

"Once there was a man who went out to sow corn. ⁴As he scattered the seed in the field, some of it fell along the path, and the birds came and ate it up. ⁵Some of it fell on rocky ground, where there was little soil. The seeds soon sprouted, because the soil wasn't deep. ⁶But when the sun came up, it burnt the young plants; and because the roots had not grown deep enough, the plants soon dried up. ⁷Some of the seed fell among thorn bushes, which grew up and choked the plants. ⁸But some seeds fell in good soil, and the plants produced corn; some produced a hundred grains, others sixty, and others thirty."

⁹And Jesus concluded, "Listen, then, if you have ears!"

22 : The Lost Son, Sheep and Coin

Luke 15.1–7

THE LOST SHEEP

¹One day when many tax collectors and other outcasts came to listen to Jesus, ²the Pharisees and the teachers of the Law started grumbling, "This man welcomes outcasts and even eats with them!" ³So Jesus told them this parable:

⁴"Suppose one of you has a hundred sheep and loses one of them—what does he do? He leaves the other ninety-nine sheep in the pasture and goes looking for the one that got lost until he finds it. ⁵When he finds it, he is so happy that he puts it on his shoulders ⁶and carries it back home. Then he calls his friends and neighbours together and says to them, 'I am so happy I found my lost sheep. Let us celebrate!' ⁷In the same way, I tell you, there will be more joy in heaven over one sinner who repents than over ninety-nine respectable people who do not need to repent.

Luke 15.8–10

THE LOST COIN

⁸"Or suppose a woman who has ten silver coins loses one of them—what does she do? She lights a lamp, sweeps her house, and looks carefully everywhere until she finds it. ⁹When she finds it, she calls her friends and neighbours together, and says to them. 'I am so happy I found the coin I lost. Let us celebrate!' ¹⁰In the same way, I tell you, the angels of God rejoice over one sinner who repents."

Luke 15.11–32

THE LOST SON

¹¹Jesus went on to say, "There was once a man who had two sons. ¹²The younger one said to him, 'Father, give me my share of the property now.' So the man divided his property between his two sons. ¹³After a few days the younger son sold his part of the property and left home with the money. He went to a country far away, where he wasted his money in reckless living. ¹⁴He spent everything he had. Then a severe famine spread over that country, and he was left without a thing. ¹⁵So he went to work for one of the citizens of that country, who sent him out to his farm to take care of the pigs. ¹⁶He wished he could fill himself with the bean pods the pigs ate, but no one gave him anything to eat. ¹⁷At last he came to his senses and said, 'All my father's hired workers have more than they can eat, and here I am about to starve! ¹⁸I will get up and go to my father and say, Father, I have sinned against God and against you. ¹⁹I am no longer fit to be called your son; treat me as one of your hired workers.' ²⁰So he got up and started back to his father.

"He was still a long way from home when his father saw him; his heart was filled with pity, and he ran, threw his arms round his son, and kissed him. ²¹'Father,' the son said, 'I have sinned against God and against you. I am no longer fit to be called your son.' ²²But the father called his servants. 'Hurry!' he said.

'Bring the best robe and put it on him. Put a ring on his finger and shoes on his feet. ²³Then go and get the prize calf and kill it, and let us celebrate with a feast! ²⁴For this son of mine was dead, but now he is alive; he was lost, but now he has been found.' And so the feasting began.

²⁵"In the meantime the elder son was out in the field. On his way back, when he came close to the house, he heard the music and dancing. ²⁶So he called one of the servants and asked him, 'What's going on?' ²⁷'Your brother has come back home,' the servant answered, 'and your father has killed the prize calf, because he got him back safe and sound.'

²⁸"The elder brother was so angry that he would not go into the house; so his father came out and begged him to come in. ²⁹But he answered his father, 'Look, all these years I have worked for you like a slave, and I have never disobeyed your orders. What have you given me? Not even a goat for me to have a feast with my friends! ³⁰But this son of yours wasted all your property on prostitutes, and when he comes back home, you kill the prize calf for him!' ³¹'My son,' the father answered, 'you are always here with me, and everything I have is yours. ³²But we had to celebrate and be happy, because your brother was dead, but now he is alive; he was lost, but now he has been found.'"

23 : The Mustard Seed and the Yeast

Matthew 13.31–32

THE MUSTARD SEED

³¹Jesus told them another parable: "The Kingdom of heaven is like this. A man takes a mustard seed and sows it in his field. ³²It is the smallest of all seeds, but when it grows up, it is the biggest of all plants. It becomes a tree, so that birds come and make their nests in its branches."

Matthew 13.33

THE YEAST

³³Jesus told them still another parable: "The Kingdom of heaven is like this. A woman takes some yeast and mixes it with forty litres of flour until the whole batch of dough rises."

24 : The Hidden Treasure and the Pearl

Matthew 13.44

THE HIDDEN TREASURE

⁴⁴"The Kingdom of heaven is like this. A man happens to find a treasure hidden in a field. He covers it up again, and is so happy that he goes and sells everything he has, and then goes back and buys that field.

Matthew 13.45–46

THE PEARL

⁴⁵"Also, the Kingdom of heaven is like this. A man is looking for fine pearls, ⁴⁶and when he finds one that is unusually fine, he goes and sells everything he has, and buys that pearl."

LIFE AND TEACHING OF JESUS

VI · Gospel extracts

25 : The Weeds and the Net

Matthew 13.24–30

THE WEEDS

²⁴Jesus told them another parable: "The Kingdom of heaven is like this. A man sowed good seed in his field. ²⁵One night, when everyone was asleep, an enemy came and sowed weeds among the wheat and went away. ²⁶When the plants grew and the ears of corn began to form, then the weeds showed up. ²⁷The man's servants came to him and said, 'Sir, it was good seed you sowed in your field; where did the weeds come from?' ²⁸'It was some enemy who did this,' he answered. 'Do you want us to go and pull up the weeds?' they asked him. ²⁹'No,' he answered, 'because as you gather the weeds you might pull up some of the wheat along with them. ³⁰Let the wheat and the weeds both grow together until harvest. Then I will tell the harvest workers to pull up the weeds first, tie them in bundles and burn them, and then to gather in the wheat and put it in my barn.'"

Matthew 13.47–50

THE NET

⁴⁷"Also, the Kingdom of heaven is like this. Some fishermen throw their net out in the lake and catch all kinds of fish. ⁴⁸When the net is full, they pull it to shore and sit down to divide the fish: the good ones go into their buckets, the worthless ones are thrown away. ⁴⁹It will be like this at the end of the age: the angels will go out and gather up the evil people from among the good ⁵⁰and will throw them into the fiery furnace, where they will cry and grind their teeth.

26 : The Three Servants

Matthew 25.14–30

¹⁴"At that time the Kingdom of heaven will be like this. Once there was a man who was about to go on a journey; he called his servants and put them in charge of his property. ¹⁵He gave to each one according to his ability: to one he gave five thousand gold coins, to another he gave two thousand, and to another he gave one thousand. Then he left on his journey. ¹⁶The servant who had received five thousand coins went at once and invested his money and earned another five thousand. ¹⁷In the same way the servant who had received two thousand coins earned another two thousand. ¹⁸But the servant who had received one thousand coins went off, dug a hole in the ground, and hid his master's money.

¹⁹"After a long time the master of those servants came back and settled accounts with them. ²⁰The servant who had received five thousand coins came in and handed over the other five thousand. 'You gave me five thousand coins, sir,' he said. 'Look! Here are another five thousand that I have earned.' ²¹'Well done, you good and faithful servant!' said his master. 'You have been faithful in managing small amounts, so I will put you in charge of large amounts. Come on in and share my happiness!'

²²"Then the servant who had been given two thousand coins came in and said, 'You gave me two thousand coins, sir. Look! Here are another two thousand that I have earned.' ²³'Well done, you good and faithful servant!' said his master. 'You have been faithful in managing small amounts, so I will put you in charge of large amounts. Come on in and share my happiness!'

²⁴"Then the servant who had received one thousand coins came in and said, 'Sir, I know you are a hard man; you reap harvests where you did not sow, and you gather crops where you did not scatter seed. ²⁵I was afraid, so I went off and hid your money in the ground. Look! Here is what belongs to you.'

²⁶"'You bad and lazy servant!' his master said. 'You knew, did you, that I reap harvests where I did not sow, and gather crops where I did not scatter seed? ²⁷Well, then, you should have deposited my money in the bank, and I would have received it all back with interest when I returned. ²⁸Now, take the money away from him and give it to the one who has ten thousand coins. ²⁹For to every person who has something, even more will be given, and he will have more than enough; but the person who has nothing, even the little that he has will be taken away from him. ³⁰As for this useless servant—throw him outside in the darkness; there he will cry and grind his teeth.'"

27 : Jesus calms a storm

Mark 4.35–41

[35]On the evening of that same day Jesus said to his disciples, "Let us go across to the other side of the lake." [36]So they left the crowd; the disciples got into the boat in which Jesus was already sitting, and they took him with them. Other boats were there too. [37]Suddenly a strong wind blew up, and the waves began to spill over into the boat, so that it was about to fill with water. [38]Jesus was in the back of the boat, sleeping with his head on a pillow. The disciples woke him up and said, "Teacher, don't you care that we are about to die?"

[39]Jesus stood up and commanded the wind, "Be quiet!" and he said to the waves, "Be still!" The wind died down, and there was a great calm. [40]Then Jesus said to his disciples, "Why are you frightened? Have you still no faith?"

[41]But they were terribly afraid and said to one another, "Who is this man? Even the wind and the waves obey him!"

28 : Jesus walks on water

Mark 6.45–51

[45]At once Jesus made his disciples get into the boat and go ahead of him to Bethsaida, on the other side of the lake, while he sent the crowd away. [46]After saying good-bye to the people he went away to a hill to pray. [47]When evening came, the boat was in the middle of the lake, while Jesus was alone on land. [48]He saw that his disciples were straining at the oars, because they were rowing against the wind; so some time between three and six o'clock in the morning he came to them, walk-

ing on the water. He was going to pass them by, [49]but they saw him walking on the water. "It's a ghost!" they thought, and screamed. [50]They were all terrified when they saw him.

Jesus spoke to them at once, "Courage!" he said. "It is I. Don't be afraid!" [51]Then he got into the boat with them, and the wind died down. The disciples were completely amazed.

29 : Jesus feeds five thousand

Mark 6.30–44

[30]The apostles returned and met with Jesus, and told him all they had done and taught. [31]There were so many people coming and going that Jesus and his disciples didn't even have time to eat. So he said to them, "Let us go off by ourselves to some place where we will be alone and you can rest for a while." [32]So they started out in a boat by themselves for a lonely place.

[33]Many people, however, saw them leave and knew at once who they were; so they went from all the towns and ran ahead by land and arrived at the place ahead of Jesus and his disciples. [34]When Jesus got out of the boat, he saw this large crowd, and his heart was filled with pity for them, because they were like sheep without a shepherd. So he began to teach them many things. [35]When it was getting late, his disciples came to him and said, "It is already very late, and this is a lonely place. [36]Send the people away, and let them go to the nearby farms and villages in order to buy themselves something to eat."

[37]"You yourselves give them something to eat," Jesus answered.

They asked, "Do you want us to go and spend two hundred silver coins on bread in order to feed them?"

[38]So Jesus asked them, "How much bread have you got? Go and see."

When they found out, they told him, "Five loaves and also two fish."

[39]Jesus then told his disciples to make all the people divide into groups and sit down on the green grass. [40]So the people sat down in rows, in groups of a hundred and groups of fifty. [41]Then Jesus took the five loaves and the two fish, looked up to heaven, and gave thanks to God. He broke the loaves and gave them to his disciples to distribute to the people. He also divided the two fish among them all. [42]Everyone ate and had enough. [43]Then the disciples took up twelve baskets full of what was left of the bread and the fish. [44]The number of men who were fed was five thousand.

30 : Jesus heals a man with evil spirits

Mark 5.1–20

¹Jesus and his disciples arrived on the other side of Lake Galilee, in the territory of Gerasa. ²As soon as Jesus got out of the boat, he was met by a man who came out of the burial caves there. This man had an evil spirit in him ³and lived among the tombs. Nobody could keep him chained up any more; ⁴many times his feet and hands had been chained, but every time he broke the chains and smashed the irons on his feet. He was too strong for anyone to control him. ⁵Day and night he wandered among the tombs and through the hills, screaming and cutting himself with stones.

⁶He was some distance away when he saw Jesus; so he ran, fell on his knees before him, ⁷and screamed in a loud voice, "Jesus, Son of the Most High God! What do you want with me? For God's sake, I beg you, don't punish me!" ⁸(He said this because Jesus was saying, "Evil spirit, come out of this man!")

⁹So Jesus asked him, "What is your name?"

The man answered, "My name is 'Mob'—there are so many of us!" ¹⁰And he kept begging Jesus not to send the evil spirits out of that region.

¹¹There was a large herd of pigs near by, feeding on a hillside. ¹²So the spirits begged Jesus, "Send us to the pigs, and let us go into them." ¹³He let them go, and the evil spirits went out of the man and entered the pigs. The whole herd—about two thousand pigs in all—rushed down the side of the cliff into the lake and was drowned.

¹⁴The men who had been taking care of the pigs ran away and spread the news in the town and among the farms. People went out to see what had happened, ¹⁵and when they came to Jesus, they saw the man who used to have the mob of demons in him. He was sitting there, clothed and in his right mind; and they were all afraid. ¹⁶Those who had seen it told the people what had happened to the man with the demons, and about the pigs.

¹⁷So they asked Jesus to leave their territory.

¹⁸As Jesus was getting into the boat, the man who had had the demons begged him, "Let me go with you!"

¹⁹But Jesus would not let him. Instead, he told him, "Go back home to your family and tell them how much the Lord has done for you and how kind he has been to you."

²⁰So the man left and went all through the Ten Towns, telling what Jesus had done for him. And all who heard it were amazed.

31 : Jairus' daughter and the woman who touched Jesus' cloak

Mark 5.21–43

²¹Jesus went back across to the other side of the lake. There at the lakeside a large crowd gathered round him. ²²Jairus, an official of the local synagogue, arrived, and when he saw Jesus, he threw himself down at his feet ²³and begged him earnestly, "My little daughter is very ill. Please come and place your hands on her, so that she will get well and live!"

²⁴Then Jesus started off with him. So many people were going along with Jesus that they were crowding him from every side.

²⁵There was a woman who had suffered terribly from severe bleeding for twelve years, ²⁶even though she had been treated by many doctors. She had spent all her money, but instead of getting better she got worse all the time. ²⁷She had heard about Jesus, so she came in the crowd behind him, ²⁸saying to herself, "If I just touch his clothes, I will get well."

²⁹She touched his cloak, and her bleeding stopped at once; and she had the feeling inside herself that she was healed of her trouble. ³⁰At once Jesus knew that power had gone out of him, so he turned round in the crowd and asked, "Who touched my clothes?"

³¹His disciples answered, "You see how the people are crowding you; why do you ask who touched you?"

³²But Jesus kept looking round to see who had done it. ³³The woman realized what had happened to her, so she came, trembling with fear, knelt at his feet, and told him the whole truth. ³⁴Jesus said to her, "My daughter, your faith has made you well. Go in peace, and be healed of your trouble."

³⁵While Jesus was saying this, some messengers came from Jairus' house and told him, "Your daughter has died. Why bother the Teacher any longer?"

³⁶Jesus paid no attention to what they said, but told him, "Don't be afraid, only believe." ³⁷Then he did not let anyone else go on with him except Peter and James and his brother John. ³⁸They arrived at Jairus' house, where Jesus saw the confusion and heard all the loud crying and wailing. ³⁹He went in and said to them, "Why all this confusion? Why are you crying? The child is not dead — she is only sleeping!"

⁴⁰They laughed at him, so he put them all out, took the child's father and mother and his three disciples, and went into the room where the child was lying. ⁴¹He took her by the hand and said to her, *"Talitha, koum,"* which means, "Little girl, I tell you to get up!"

⁴²She got up at once and started walking around. (She was twelve years old.) When this happened, they were completely amazed. ⁴³But Jesus gave them strict orders not to tell anyone, and he said, "Give her something to eat."

32 : A woman's faith

Mark 7.24–30

²⁴Then Jesus left and went away to the territory near the city of Tyre. He went into a house and did not want anyone to know he was there, but he could not stay hidden. ²⁵A woman, whose daughter had an evil spirit in her, heard about Jesus and came to him at once and fell at his feet. ²⁶The woman was a Gentile, born in the region of Phoenicia in Syria. She begged Jesus to drive the demon out of her daughter. ²⁷But Jesus answered, "Let us first feed the children. It isn't right to take the children's food and throw it to the dogs."

²⁸"Sir," she answered, "even the dogs under the table eat the children's leftovers!"

²⁹So Jesus said to her, "Because of that answer, go back home, where you will find that the demon has gone out of your daughter!"

³⁰She went home and found her child lying on the bed; the demon had indeed gone out of her.

33 : Blind Bartimaeus

Mark 10.46–52

⁴⁶They came to Jericho, and as Jesus was leaving with his disciples and a large crowd, a blind beggar named Bartimaeus son of Timaeus was sitting by the road. ⁴⁷When he heard that it was Jesus of Nazareth, he began to shout, "Jesus! Son of David! Take pity on me!"

⁴⁸Many of the people scolded him and told him to be quiet. But he shouted even more loudly, "Son of David, take pity on me!"

⁴⁹Jesus stopped and said, "Call him."

So they called the blind man. "Cheer up!" they said. "Get up, he is calling you."

⁵⁰He threw off his cloak, jumped up, and came to Jesus.

⁵¹"What do you want me to do for you?" Jesus asked him.

"Teacher," the blind man answered, "I want to see again."

⁵²"Go," Jesus told him, "your faith has made you well."

At once he was able to see and followed Jesus on the road.

34 : The Roman officer's servant

Luke 7.1–10

¹When Jesus had finished saying all these things to the people, he went to Capernaum. ²A Roman officer there had a servant who was very dear to him; the man was sick and about to die. ³When the officer heard about Jesus, he sent some Jewish elders to ask him to come and heal his servant. ⁴They came to Jesus and begged him earnestly, "This man really deserves your help. ⁵He loves our people and he himself built a synagogue for us."

⁶So Jesus went with them. He was not far from the house when the officer sent friends to tell him, "Sir, don't trouble yourself. I do not deserve to have you come into my house, ⁷neither do I consider myself worthy to come to you in person. Just give the order, and my servant will get well. ⁸I, too, am a man placed under the authority of superior officers, and I have soldiers under me. I order this one, 'Go!' and he goes; I order that one, 'Come!' and he comes; and I order my slave, 'Do this!' and he does it."

⁹Jesus was surprised when he heard this; he turned round and said to the crowd following him, "I tell you, I have never found faith like this, not even in Israel!"

¹⁰The messengers went back to the officer's house and found his servant well.

35 : Jesus heals ten men

Luke 17.11–19

[11]As Jesus made his way to Jerusalem, he went along the border between Samaria and Galilee. [12]He was going into a village when he was met by ten men suffering from a dreaded skin-disease. They stood at a distance [13]and shouted, "Jesus! Master! Take pity on us!"

[14]Jesus saw them and said to them, "Go and let the priests examine you."

On the way they were made clean. [15]When one of them saw that he was healed, he came back, praising God in a loud voice. [16]He threw himself to the ground at Jesus' feet and thanked him. The man was a Samaritan. [17]Jesus said, "There were ten men who were healed; where are the other nine? [18]Why is this foreigner the only one who came back to give thanks to God?" [19]And Jesus said to him, "Get up and go; your faith has made you well."

36 : Jesus raises a widow's son

Luke 7.11–17

[11]Soon afterwards Jesus went to a town called Nain, accompanied by his disciples and a large crowd. [12]Just as he arrived at the gate of the town, a funeral procession was coming out. The dead man was the only son of a woman who was a widow, and a large crowd from the town was with her. [13]When the Lord saw her, his heart was filled with pity for her, and he said to her, "Don't cry." [14]Then he walked over and touched the coffin, and the men carrying it stopped. Jesus said, "Young man! Get up. I tell you!" [15]The dead man sat up and began to talk, and Jesus gave him back to his mother.

[16]They all were filled with fear and praised God. "A great prophet has appeared among us!" they said; "God has come to save his people!"

[17]This news about Jesus went out through all the country and the surrounding territory.

37 : Triumphant entry into Jerusalem

Luke 19.28–40

[28]Jesus said this and then went on to Jerusalem ahead of them. [29]As he came near Bethphage and Bethany at the Mount of Olives, he sent two disciples ahead [30]with these instructions: "Go to the village there ahead of you; as you go in, you will find a colt tied up that has never been ridden. Untie it and bring it here. [31]If someone asks you why you are untying it, tell him that the Master needs it."

[32]They went on their way and found everything just as Jesus had told them. [33]As they were untying the colt, its owners said to them, "Why are you untying it?"

[34]"The Master needs it," they answered, [35]and they took the colt to Jesus. Then they threw their cloaks over the animal and helped Jesus get on. [36]As he rode on, people spread their cloaks on the road.

[37]When he came near Jerusalem, at the place where the road went down the Mount of Olives, the large crowd of his disciples began to thank God and praise him in loud voices for all the great things that they had seen: [38]"God bless the king who comes in the name of the Lord! Peace in heaven and glory to God!"

[39]Then some of the Pharisees in the crowd spoke to Jesus. "Teacher," they said, "command your disciples to be quiet!"

[40]Jesus answered, "I tell you that if they keep quiet, the stones themselves will start shouting."

38: Jesus goes into the Temple

Mark 11.15–19

¹⁵When they arrived in Jerusalem, Jesus went to the Temple and began to drive out all those who were buying and selling. He overturned the tables of the money-changers and the stools of those who sold pigeons, ¹⁶and he would not let anyone carry anything through the temple courtyards. ¹⁷He then taught the people: "It is written in the Scriptures that God said, 'My Temple will be called a house of prayer for the people of all nations.' But you have turned it into a hideout for thieves!"

¹⁸The chief priests and the teachers of the Law heard of this, so they began looking for some way to kill Jesus. They were afraid of him, because the whole crowd was amazed at his teaching.

¹⁹When evening came, Jesus and his disciples left the city.

39: The question about Jesus' authority

Mark 11.27–33

²⁷They arrived once again in Jerusalem. As Jesus was walking in the Temple, the chief priests, the teachers of the Law, and the elders came to him ²⁸and asked him, "What right have you to do these things? Who gave you this right?"

²⁹Jesus answered them, "I will ask you just one question, and if you give me an answer, I will tell you what right I have to do these things. ³⁰Tell me, where did John's right to baptize come from: was it from God or from man?"

³¹They started to argue among themselves: "What shall we say? If we answer, 'From God,' he will say, 'Why, then, did you not believe John?' ³²But if we say, 'From man ...'" (They were afraid of the people, because everyone was convinced that John had been a prophet.) ³³So their answer to Jesus was, "We don't know."

Jesus said to them, "Neither will I tell you, then, by what right I do these things."

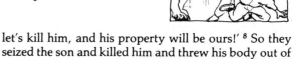

40: The parable of the Tenants in the Vineyard

Mark 12.1–12

¹Then Jesus spoke to them in parables: "Once there was a man who planted a vineyard, put a fence round it, dug a hole for the winepress, and built a watch-tower. Then he let out the vineyard to tenants and left home on a journey. ²When the time came to gather the grapes, he sent a slave to the tenants to receive from them his share of the harvest. ³The tenants seized the slave, beat him, and sent him back without a thing. ⁴Then the owner sent another slave; the tenants beat him over the head and treated him shamefully. ⁵The owner sent another slave, and they killed him; and they treated many others the same way, beating some and killing others. ⁶The only one left to send was the man's own dear son. Last of all, then, he sent his son to the tenants. 'I am sure they will respect my son,' he said. ⁷But those tenants said to one another, 'This is the owner's son. Come on, let's kill him, and his property will be ours!' ⁸ So they seized the son and killed him and threw his body out of the vineyard.

⁹"What, then, will the owner of the vineyard do?" asked Jesus. "He will come and kill those men and hand the vineyard over to other tenants. ¹⁰Surely you have read this scripture?

'The stone which the builders rejected as worthless turned out to be the most important of all.

¹¹This was done by the Lord;
   what a wonderful sight it is!'"

¹²The Jewish leaders tried to arrest Jesus, because they knew that he had told this parable against them. But they were afraid of the crowd, so they left him and went away.

41 : The question about paying taxes

Mark 12.13–17

¹³Some Pharisees and some members of Herod's party were sent to Jesus to trap him with questions. ¹⁴They came to him and said, "Teacher, we know that you tell the truth, without worrying about what people think. You pay no attention to a man's status, but teach the truth about God's will for man. Tell us, is it against our Law to pay taxes to the Roman Emperor? Should we pay them or not?"

¹⁵But Jesus saw through their trick and answered,

"Why are you trying to trap me? Bring a silver coin, and let me see it."

¹⁶They brought him one, and he asked, "Whose face and name are these?"

"The Emperor's," they answered.

¹⁷So Jesus said, "Well, then, pay the Emperor what belongs to the Emperor, and pay God what belongs to God."

And they were amazed at Jesus.

42 : Jesus warns against the teachers of the Law

Mark 12.38–40

A large crowd was listening to Jesus gladly. ³⁸As he taught them, he said, "Watch out for the teachers of the Law, who like to walk around in their long robes and be greeted with respect in the market-place, ³⁹who choose the reserved seats in the synagogues and the best places at feasts. ⁴⁰They take advantage of widows and rob them of their homes, and then make a show of saying long prayers. Their punishment will be all the worse!"

43 : The widow's offering

Mark 12.41–44

⁴¹As Jesus sat near the temple treasury, he watched the people as they dropped in their money. Many rich men dropped in a lot of money; ⁴²then a poor widow came along and dropped in two little copper coins, worth about a penny. ⁴³He called his disciples together and said to them, "I tell you that this poor widow put more in the offering box than all the others. ⁴⁴For the others put in what they had to spare of their riches; but she, poor as she is, put in all she had—she gave all she had to live on."

44 : The plot against Jesus

Mark 14.1–2

¹It was now two days before the Festival of Passover and Unleavened Bread. The chief priests and the teachers of the Law were looking for a way to arrest Jesus secretly and put him to death. ²"We must not do it during the festival," they said, "or the people might riot."

45 : Jesus is anointed at Bethany

Mark 14.3–9

³Jesus was in Bethany at the house of Simon, a man who had suffered from a dreaded skin-disease. While Jesus was eating, a woman came in with an alabaster jar full of a very expensive perfume made of pure nard. She broke the jar and poured the perfume on Jesus' head. ⁴Some of the people there became angry and said to one another, "What was the use of wasting the perfume? ⁵It could have been sold for more than three hundred silver coins and the money given to the poor!" And they criticized her harshly.

⁶But Jesus said, "Leave her alone! Why are you bothering her? She has done a fine and beautiful thing for me. ⁷You will always have poor people with you, and any time you want to, you can help them. But you will not always have me. ⁸She did what she could; she poured perfume on my body to prepare it ahead of time for burial. ⁹Now, I assure you that wherever the gospel is preached all over the world, what she has done will be told in memory of her."

LIFE AND TEACHING OF JESUS

VI · Gospel extracts

46: Judas agrees to betray Jesus

Mark 14.10–11

¹⁰Then Judas Iscariot, one of the twelve disciples, went off to the chief priests in order to betray Jesus to them. ¹¹They were pleased to hear what he had to say, and promised to give him money. So Judas started looking for a good chance to hand Jesus over to them.

47: Jesus eats the Passover meal with his disciples

Mark 14.12–16

¹²On the first day of the Festival of Unleavened Bread, the day the lambs for the Passover meal were killed, Jesus' disciples asked him, 'Where do you want us to go and get the Passover meal ready for you?'

¹³Then Jesus sent two of them with these instructions: 'Go into the city, and a man carrying a jar of water will meet you. Follow him ¹⁴to the house he enters, and say to the owner of the house: 'The Teacher says, Where is the room where my disciples and I will eat the Passover meal?' ¹⁵Then he will show you a large upstairs room, prepared and furnished, where you will get everything ready for us.'

¹⁶The disciples left, went to the city, and found everything just as Jesus had told them; and they prepared the Passover meal.

48: The Last Supper (1)

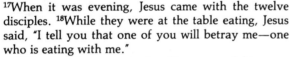

Mark 14.17–21

¹⁷When it was evening, Jesus came with the twelve disciples. ¹⁸While they were at the table eating, Jesus said, 'I tell you that one of you will betray me—one who is eating with me.'

¹⁹The disciples were upset and began to ask him, one after the other, 'Surely you don't mean me, do you?'

²⁰Jesus answered, 'It will be one of you twelve, one who dips his bread in the dish with me. ²¹The Son of Man will die as the Scriptures say he will; but how terrible for that man who betrays the Son of Man! It would have been better for that man if he had never been born!'

49: The Last Supper (2)

Mark 14.22–26

²²While they were eating, Jesus took a piece of bread, gave a prayer of thanks, broke it, and gave it to his disciples. 'Take it,' he said, 'this is my body.'

²³Then he took a cup, gave thanks to God, and handed it to them; and they all drank from it. ²⁴Jesus said, 'This is my blood which is poured out for many, my blood which seals God's covenant. ²⁵I tell you, I will never again drink this wine until the day I drink the new wine in the Kingdom of God.'

²⁶Then they sang a hymn and went out to the Mount of Olives.

50: Jesus predicts Peter's denial

Mark 14.27–31

²⁷Jesus said to them, 'All of you will run away and leave me, for the scripture says, 'God will kill the shepherd, and the sheep will be all scattered.' ²⁸But after I am raised to life, I will go to Galilee ahead of you.'

²⁹Peter answered, 'I will never leave you, even though all the rest do!'

³⁰Jesus said to Peter, 'I tell you that before the cock crows twice tonight, you will say three times that you do not know me.'

³¹Peter answered even more strongly, 'I will never say that, even if I have to die with you!'

And all the other disciples said the same thing.

51 : Jesus prays in Gethsemane

Mark 14.32–42

³²They came to a place called Gethsemane, and Jesus said to his disciples, "Sit here while I pray." ³³He took Peter, James, and John with him. Distress and anguish came over him, ³⁴and he said to them, "The sorrow in my heart is so great that it almost crushes me. Stay here and keep watch."

³⁵He went a little farther on, threw himself on the ground, and prayed that, if possible, he might not have to go through that time of suffering. ³⁶"Father," he prayed, "my Father! All things are possible for you. Take this cup of suffering away from me. Yet not what I want, but what you want."

³⁷Then he returned and found the three disciples asleep. He said to Peter, "Simon, are you asleep? Weren't you able to stay awake even for one hour?" ³⁸And he said to them, "Keep watch, and pray that you will not fall into temptation. The spirit is willing, but the flesh is weak."

³⁹He went away once more and prayed, saying the same words. ⁴⁰Then he came back to the disciples and found them asleep; they could not keep their eyes open. And they did not know what to say to him.

⁴¹When he came back the third time, he said to them, "Are you still sleeping and resting? Enough! The hour has come! Look, the Son of Man is now being handed over to the power of sinful men. ⁴²Get up, let us go. Look, here is the man who is betraying me!"

52 : The trial before the High Priest

Matthew 26.57–68

⁵⁷Those who had arrested Jesus took him to the house of Caiaphas, the High Priest, where the teachers of the Law and the elders had gathered together. ⁵⁸Peter followed from a distance, as far as the courtyard of the High Priest's house. He went into the courtyard and sat down with the guards to see how it would all come out. ⁵⁹The chief priests and the whole Council tried to find some false evidence against Jesus to put him to death; ⁶⁰but they could not find any, even though many people came forward and told lies about him. Finally two men stepped up ⁶¹and said, "This man said, 'I am able to tear down God's Temple and three days later build it up again.'"

⁶²The High Priest stood up and said to Jesus, "Have you no answer to give to this accusation against you?" ⁶³But Jesus kept quiet. Again the High Priest spoke to him, "In the name of the living God I now put you on oath: tell us if you are the Messiah, the Son of God."

⁶⁴Jesus answered him, "So you say. But I tell all of you: from this time on you will see the Son of Man sitting on the right of the Almighty and coming on the clouds of heaven!"

⁶⁵At this the High Priest tore his clothes and said, "Blasphemy! We don't need any more witnesses! You have just heard his blasphemy! ⁶⁶What do you think?"

They answered, "He is guilty and must die."

⁶⁷Then they spat in his face and beat him; and those who slapped him ⁶⁸said, "Prophesy for us, Messiah! Guess who hit you!"

Mark 14.53–65

⁵³Then Jesus was taken to the High Priest's house, where all the chief priests, the elders, and the teachers of the Law were gathering. ⁵⁴Peter followed from a distance and went into the courtyard of the High Priest's house. There he sat down with the guards, keeping himself warm by the fire. ⁵⁵The chief priests and the whole Council tried to find some evidence against Jesus in order to put him to death; but they could not find any. ⁵⁶Many witnesses told lies against Jesus, but their stories did not agree.

⁵⁷Then some men stood up and told this lie against Jesus: ⁵⁸"We heard him say, 'I will tear down this Temple which men have made, and after three days I will build one that is not made by men.'" ⁵⁹Not even they, however, could make their stories agree.

⁶⁰The High Priest stood up in front of them all and questioned Jesus, "Have you no answer to the accusation they bring against you?"

⁶¹But Jesus kept quiet and would not say a word. Again the High Priest questioned him, "Are you the Messiah, the Son of the Blessed God?"

⁶²"I am," answered Jesus, "and you will all see the Son of Man seated on the right of the Almighty and coming with the clouds of heaven!"

⁶³The High Priest tore his robes and said, "We don't need any more witnesses! ⁶⁴You heard his blasphemy. What is your decision?"

They all voted against him: he was guilty and should be put to death.

⁶⁵Some of them began to spit on Jesus, and they blindfolded him and hit him. "Guess who hit you!" they said. And the guards took him and slapped him.

Luke 22.66–71

⁶⁶When day came, the elders, the chief priests, and the teachers of the Law met together, and Jesus was brought before the Council. ⁶⁷"Tell us," they said, "are you the Messiah?"

He answered, "If I tell you, you will not believe me; ⁶⁸and if I ask you a question, you will not answer. ⁶⁹But from now on the Son of Man will be seated on the right of Almighty God."

⁷⁰They all said, "Are you, then, the Son of God?"

He answered them, "You say that I am."

⁷¹And they said, "We don't need any witnesses! We ourselves have heard what he said!"

53 : Peter's denial

Mark 14.66–72

⁶⁶Peter was still down in the courtyard when one of the High Priest's servant-girls came by. ⁶⁷When she saw Peter warming himself, she looked straight at him and said, "You, too, were with Jesus of Nazareth."

⁶⁸But he denied it. "I don't know . . . I don't understand what you are talking about," he answered, and went out into the passage. Just then a cock crowed.

⁶⁹The servant-girl saw him there and began to repeat to the bystanders, "He is one of them!" ⁷⁰But Peter denied it again.

A little while later the bystanders accused Peter again, "You can't deny that you are one of them, because you, too, are from Galilee."

⁷¹Then Peter said, "I swear that I am telling the truth! May God punish me if I am not! I do not know the man you are talking about!"

⁷²Just then a cock crowed a second time, and Peter remembered how Jesus had said to him, "Before the cock crows twice, you will say three times that you do not know me." And he broke down and cried.

54 : Jesus is brought before Pilate

Mark 15.1–5

¹Early in the morning the chief priests met hurriedly with the elders, the teachers of the Law, and the whole Council, and made their plans. They put Jesus in chains, led him away, and handed him over to Pilate. ²Pilate questioned him, "Are you the king of the Jews?"

Jesus answered, "So you say."

³The chief priests were accusing Jesus of many things, ⁴so Pilate questioned him again, "Aren't you going to answer? Listen to all their accusations!"

⁵Again Jesus refused to say a word, and Pilate was amazed.

Luke 23.1–5

¹The whole group rose up and took Jesus before Pilate, ²where they began to accuse him: "We caught this man misleading our people, telling them not to pay taxes to the Emperor and claiming that he himself is the Messiah, a king."

³Pilate asked him, "Are you the king of the Jews?"

"So you say," answered Jesus.

⁴Then Pilate said to the chief priests and the crowds, "I find no reason to condemn this man."

⁵But they insisted even more strongly, "With his teaching he is starting a riot among the people all through Judaea. He began in Galilee and now has come here."

55 : Jesus is sentenced to death

Mark 15.6–15

⁶At every Passover Festival Pilate was in the habit of setting free any one prisoner the people asked for. ⁷At that time a man named Barabbas was in prison with the rebels who had committed murder in the riot. ⁸When the crowd gathered and began to ask Pilate for the usual favour, ⁹he asked them, "Do you want me to set free for you the king of the Jews?" ¹⁰He knew very well that the chief priests had handed Jesus over to him because they were jealous.

¹¹But the chief priests stirred up the crowd to ask,

instead, for Pilate to set Barabbas free for them. ¹²Pilate spoke again to the crowd, "What, then, do you want me to do with the one you call the king of the Jews?"

¹³They shouted back, "Crucify him!"

¹⁴"But what crime has he committed?" Pilate asked. They shouted all the louder, "Crucify him!"

¹⁵Pilate wanted to please the crowd, so he set Barabbas free for them. Then he had Jesus whipped and handed him over to be crucified.

56: The soldiers mock Jesus

Mark 15.16–20

¹⁶The soldiers took Jesus inside to the courtyard of the governor's palace and called together the rest of the company. ¹⁷They put a purple robe on Jesus, made a crown out of thorny branches, and put it on his head. ¹⁸Then they began to salute him: "Long live the King of the Jews!"¹⁹They beat him over the head with a stick, spat on him, fell on their knees, and bowed down to him. ²⁰When they had finished mocking him, they took off the purple robe and put his own clothes back on him. Then they led him out to crucify him.

57: The Crucifixion

Mark 15.21–27, 29–32

²¹On the way they met a man named Simon, who was coming into the city from the country, and the soldiers forced him to carry Jesus' cross. (Simon was from Cyrene and was the father of Alexander and Rufus.) ²²They took Jesus to a place called Golgotha, which means "The Place of the Skull." ²³There they tried to give him wine mixed with a drug called myrrh, but Jesus would not drink it. ²⁴Then they crucified him and divided his clothes among themselves, throwing dice to see who would get which piece of clothing. ²⁵It was nine o'clock in the morning when they crucified him. ²⁶The notice of the accusation against him said: "The King of the Jews." ²⁷They also crucified two bandits with Jesus, one on his right and the other on his left.

²⁹People passing by shook their heads and hurled insults at Jesus: "Aha! You were going to tear down the Temple and build it up again in three days! ³⁰Now come down from the cross and save yourself!"

³¹In the same way the chief priests and the teachers of the Law jeered at Jesus, saying to each other, "He saved others, but he cannot save himself! ³²Let us see the Messiah, the king of Israel, come down from the cross now, and we will believe in him!"

And the two who were crucified with Jesus insulted him also.

Matthew 27.32–44

³²As they were going out, they met a man from Cyrene named Simon, and the soldiers forced him to carry Jesus' cross. ³³They came to a place called Golgotha, which means, "The Place of the Skull." ³⁴There they offered Jesus wine mixed with a bitter substance; but after tasting it, he would not drink it.

³⁵They crucified him and then divided his clothes among them by throwing dice. ³⁶After that they sat there and watched him. ³⁷Above his head they put the written notice of the accusation against him: "This is Jesus, the King of the Jews." ³⁸Then they crucified two bandits with Jesus, one on his right and the other on his left.

³⁹People passing by shook their heads and hurled insults at Jesus: ⁴⁰"You were going to tear down the Temple and build it up again in three days! Save yourself if you are God's Son! Come on down from the cross!"

⁴¹In the same way the chief priests and the teachers of the Law and the elders jeered at him: ⁴²"He saved others, but he cannot save himself! Isn't he the king of Israel? If he comes down off the cross now, we will believe in him! ⁴³He trusts in God and claims to be God's Son. Well, then, let us see if God wants to save him now!"

⁴⁴Even the bandits who had been crucified with him insulted him in the same way.

Luke 23.26–43

²⁶The soldiers led Jesus away, and as they were going, they met a man from Cyrene named Simon who was coming into the city from the country. They seized him, put the cross on him, and made him carry it behind Jesus.

²⁷A large crowd of people followed him; among them were some women who were weeping and wailing for him. ²⁸Jesus turned to them and said, "Women of Jerusalem! Don't cry for me, but for yourselves and your children. ²⁹For the days are coming when people will say 'How lucky are the women who never had children, who never bore babies, who never nursed them!' ³⁰That will be the time when people will say to the mountains, 'Fall on us!' and to the hills, 'Hide us!' ³¹For if such things as these are done when the wood is green, what will happen when it is dry?"

³²Two other men, both of them criminals, were also led out to be put to death with Jesus. ³³When they came to the place called "The Skull," they crucified Jesus there, and the two criminals, one on his right and the other on his left. ³⁴Jesus said, "Forgive them, Father! They don't know what they are doing."

They divided his clothes among themselves by throwing dice. ³⁵The people stood there watching while the Jewish leaders jeered at him: "He saved others; let him save himself if he is the Messiah whom God has chosen!"

³⁶The soldiers also mocked him: they came up to him and offered him cheap wine, ³⁷and said, "Save yourself if you are the king of the Jews!"

³⁸Above him were written these words: "This is the King of the Jews."

³⁹One of the criminals hanging there hurled insults at him: "Aren't you the Messiah? Save yourself and us!"

⁴⁰The other one, however, rebuked him, saying "Don't you fear God? You received the same sentence he did. ⁴¹Ours, however, is only right, because we are getting what we deserve for what we did; but he has done no wrong." ⁴²And he said to Jesus, "Remember me, Jesus, when you come as King!"

⁴³Jesus said to him, "I promise you that today you will be in Paradise with me."

58: The Death of Jesus

Mark 15.33–41

³³At noon the whole country was covered with darkness, which lasted for three hours. ³⁴At three o'clock Jesus cried out with a loud shout, "*Eloi, Eloi, lema sabachthani?*" which means, "My God, my God, why did you abandon me?"

³⁵Some of the people there heard him and said, "Listen, he is calling for Elijah!" ³⁶One of them ran up with a sponge, soaked it in cheap wine, and put it on the end of a stick. Then he held it up to Jesus' lips and said, "Wait! Let us see if Elijah is coming to bring him down from the cross!"

³⁷With a loud cry Jesus died.

³⁸The curtain hanging in the Temple was torn in two, from top to bottom. ³⁹The army officer who was standing there in front of the cross saw how Jesus had died. "This man was really the Son of God!" he said.

⁴⁰Some women were there, looking on from a distance. Among them were Mary Magdalene, Mary the mother of the younger James and of Joseph, and Salome. ⁴¹They had followed Jesus while he was in Galilee and had helped him. Many other women who had come to Jerusalem with him were there also.

Luke 23.44–49

⁴⁴It was about twelve o'clock when the sun stopped shining and darkness covered the whole country until three o'clock; ⁴⁵and the curtain hanging in the Temple was torn in two. ⁴⁶Jesus cried out in a loud voice, "Father! In your hands I place my spirit!" He said this and died.

⁴⁷The army officer saw what had happened, and he praised God, saying, "Certainly he was a good man!"

⁴⁸When the people who had gathered there to watch the spectacle saw what happened, they all went back home, beating their breasts in sorrow. ⁴⁹All those who knew Jesus personally, including the women who had followed him from Galilee, stood at a distance to watch.

Matthew 27.45–56

⁴⁵At noon the whole country was covered with darkness, which lasted for three hours. ⁴⁶At about three o'clock Jesus cried out with a loud shout, "*Eli, Eli, lema sabachthani?*" which means, "My God, my God, why did you abandon me?"

⁴⁷Some of the people standing there heard him and said, "He is calling for Elijah!" ⁴⁸One of them ran up at once, took a sponge, soaked it in cheap wine, put it on the end of a stick, and tried to make him drink it.

⁴⁹But the others said, "Wait, let us see if Elijah is coming to save him!"

⁵⁰Jesus again gave a loud cry and breathed his last.

⁵¹Then the curtain hanging in the Temple was torn in two from top to bottom. The earth shook, the rocks split apart, ⁵²the graves broke open, and many of God's people who had died were raised to life. ⁵³They left the graves, and after Jesus rose from death, they went into the Holy City, where many people saw them.

⁵⁴When the army officer and the soldiers with him who were watching Jesus saw the earthquake and everything else that happened, they were terrified and said, "He really was the Son of God!"

⁵⁵There were many women there, looking on from a distance, who had followed Jesus from Galilee and helped him. ⁵⁶Among them were Mary Magdalene, Mary the mother of James and Joseph, and the wife of Zebedee.

59 : The Burial of Jesus

Luke 23.50–56

⁵⁰⁻⁵¹There was a man named Joseph from Arimathea, a town in Judaea. He was a good and honourable man, who was waiting for the coming of the Kingdom of God. Although he was a member of the Council, he had not agreed with their decision and action. ⁵²He went into the presence of Pilate and asked for the body of Jesus. ⁵³Then he took the body down, wrapped it in a linen sheet, and placed it in a tomb which had been dug out of solid rock and which had never been used. ⁵⁴It was Friday, and the Sabbath was about to begin.

⁵⁵The women who had followed Jesus from Galilee went with Joseph and saw the tomb and how Jesus' body was placed in it. ⁵⁶Then they went back home and prepared the spices and perfumes for the body.

On the Sabbath they rested, as the Law commanded.

Mark 15.42–47

⁴²⁻⁴³It was towards evening when Joseph of Arimathea arrived. He was a respected member of the Council, who was waiting for the coming of the Kingdom of God. It was Preparation day (that is, the day before the Sabbath), so Joseph went boldly into the presence of Pilate and asked him for the body of Jesus. ⁴⁴Pilate was surprised to hear that Jesus was already dead. He called the army officer and asked him if Jesus had been dead a long time. ⁴⁵After hearing the officer's report, Pilate told Joseph he could have the body. ⁴⁶Joseph bought a linen sheet, took the body down, wrapped it in the sheet, and placed it in a tomb which had been dug out of solid rock. Then he rolled a large stone across the entrance to the tomb. ⁴⁷Mary Magdalene and Mary the mother of Joseph were watching and saw where the body of Jesus was placed.

Matthew 27.57–61

⁵⁷When it was evening, a rich man from Arimathea arrived; his name was Joseph, and he also was a disciple of Jesus. ⁵⁸He went into the presence of Pilate and asked for the body of Jesus. Pilate gave orders for the body to be given to Joseph. ⁵⁹So Joseph took it, wrapped it in a new linen sheet, ⁶⁰and placed it in his own tomb, which he had just recently dug out of solid rock. Then he rolled a large stone across the entrance to the tomb and went away. ⁶¹Mary Magdalene and the other Mary were sitting there, facing the tomb.

60 : The Resurrection

Matthew 28.1–10

¹After the Sabbath, as Sunday morning was dawning, Mary Magdalene and the other Mary went to look at the tomb. ²Suddenly there was a violent earthquake; an angel of the Lord came down from heaven, rolled the stone away, and sat on it. ³His appearance was like lightning, and his clothes were white as snow. ⁴The guards were so afraid that they trembled and became like dead men.

⁵The angel spoke to the women. "You must not be afraid," he said. "I know you are looking for Jesus, who was crucified. ⁶He is not here; he has been raised, just as he said. Come here and see the place where he was lying. ⁷Go quickly now, and tell his disciples, 'He has been raised from death, and now he is going to Galilee ahead of you; there you will see him!' Remember what I have told you."

⁸So they left the tomb in a hurry, afraid and yet filled with joy, and ran to tell his disciples.

⁹Suddenly Jesus met them and said, "Peace be with you." They came up to him, took hold of his feet, and worshipped him. ¹⁰"Do not be afraid," Jesus said to them. "Go and tell my brothers to go to Galilee, and there they will see me."

Mark 16.1–8

¹After the Sabbath was over, Mary Magdalene, Mary the mother of James, and Salome bought spices to go and anoint the body of Jesus. ²Very early on Sunday morning, at sunrise, they went to the tomb. ³⁻⁴On the way they said to one another, "Who will roll away the stone for us from the entrance to the tomb?" (It was a very large stone.) Then they looked up and saw that the stone had already been rolled back. ⁵So they entered the tomb, where they saw a young man sitting on the right, wearing a white robe—and they were alarmed.

⁶"Don't be alarmed," he said. "I know you are looking for Jesus of Nazareth, who was crucified. He is not here—he has been raised! Look, here is the place where they put him. ⁷Now go and give this message to his disciples, including Peter: 'He is going to Galilee ahead of you; there you will see him, just as he told you.'"

⁸So they went out and ran from the tomb, distressed and terrified. They said nothing to anyone, because they were afraid.

(More extracts on page 84)

LIFE AND TEACHING OF JESUS

VI · Gospel extracts

¹Very early on Sunday morning the women went to the tomb, carrying the spices they had prepared. ²They found the stone rolled away from the entrance to the tomb, ³so they went in; but they did not find the body of the Lord Jesus. ⁴They stood there puzzled about this, when suddenly two men in bright shining clothes stood by them. ⁵Full of fear, the women bowed down to the ground, as the men said to them, "Why are you looking among the dead for one who is alive? ⁶He is not here; he has been raised. Remember what he said to you while he was in Galilee: ⁷'The Son of Man must be handed over to sinful men, be crucified, and three days later rise to life.'"

⁸Then the women remembered his words, ⁹returned from the tomb, and told all these things to the eleven disciples and all the rest. ¹⁰The women were Mary Magdalene, Joanna, and Mary the mother of James; they and the other women with them told these things to the apostles. ¹¹But the apostles thought that what the women said was nonsense, and they did not believe them. ¹²But Peter got up and ran to the tomb; he bent down and saw the linen wrappings but nothing else. Then he went back home amazed at what had happened.

Luke 24.13–35

THE WALK TO EMMAUS

¹³On that same day two of Jesus' followers were going to a village named Emmaus, about eleven kilometres from Jerusalem, ¹⁴and they were talking to each other about all the things that had happened. ¹⁵As they talked and discussed, Jesus himself drew near and walked along with them; ¹⁶they saw him, but somehow did not recognize him. ¹⁷Jesus said to them, "What are you talking about to each other, as you walk along?"

They stood still, with sad faces. ¹⁸One of them, named Cleopas, asked him, "Are you the only visitor in Jerusalem who doesn't know the things that have been happening there these last few days?"

¹⁹"What things?" he asked.

"The things that happened to Jesus of Nazareth," they answered. "This man was a prophet and was considered by God and by all the people to be powerful in everything he said and did. ²⁰Our chief priests and rulers handed him over to be sentenced to death, and he was crucified. ²¹And we had hoped that he would be the one who was going to set Israel free! Besides all that, this is now the third day since it happened. ²²Some of the women of our group surprised us, they went at dawn to the tomb, ²³but could not find his body. They came back saying they had seen a vision of angels who told them that he is alive. ²⁴Some of our group went to the tomb and found it exactly as the women had said, but they did not see him."

²⁵Then Jesus said to them, "How foolish you are, how slow you are to believe everything the prophets said! ²⁶Was it not necessary for the Messiah to suffer these things and then to enter his glory?" ²⁷And Jesus explained to them what was said about himself in all the Scriptures, beginning with the books of Moses and the writings of all the prophets.

²⁸As they came near the village to which they were going, Jesus acted as if he were going farther; ²⁹but they held him back, saying, "Stay with us; the day is almost over and it is getting dark." So he went in to stay with them. ³⁰He sat down to eat with them, took the bread, and said the blessing; then he broke the bread and gave it to them. ³¹Then their eyes were opened and they recognized him, but he disappeared from their sight. ³²They said to each other, "Wasn't it like a fire burning in us when he talked to us on the road and explained the Scriptures to us?"

³³They got up at once and went back to Jerusalem, where they found the eleven disciples gathered together with the others ³⁴and saying, "The Lord is risen indeed! He has appeared to Simon!"

³⁵The two then explained to them what had happened on the road, and how they had recognized the Lord when he broke the bread.

61 : The Ascension

Matthew 28.16–20

JESUS APPEARS TO HIS DISCIPLES

¹⁶The eleven disciples went to the hill in Galilee where Jesus had told them to go. ¹⁷When they saw him, they worshipped him, even though some of them doubted. ¹⁸Jesus drew near and said to them, "I have been given all authority in heaven and on earth. ¹⁹Go, then, to all peoples everywhere and make them my disciples: baptize them in the name of the Father, the Son, and the Holy Spirit, ²⁰and teach them to obey everything I have commanded you. And I will be with you always, to the end of the age."

Luke 24.50–53

JESUS IS TAKEN UP TO HEAVEN

⁵⁰Then he led them out of the city as far as Bethany, where he raised his hands and blessed them. ⁵¹As he was blessing them, he departed from them and was taken up into heaven. ⁵²They worshipped him and went back into Jerusalem, filled with great joy, ⁵³and spent all their time in the Temple giving thanks to God.

Module Contract

Between student _____

and teacher _____

Topic _____

Task description	Complete all . . . . tasks on the assignment sheets forming the module. There are _____ of these.
Amount and standard	Genuine work on all the task questions. This must include neat written work and diagrams, if necessary. Headings must be underlined. Pages should be numbered. There should be a Contents page, a Book List and a cover, with title or area of study and your name.
Resources	As suggested by your teacher/tutor, try to find suitable materials from the resources centre.
Planning deadline	All work to be handed in fully completed on
Assessment	Tasks to be assessed as previously indicated—Knowledge, Understanding and Evaluation.
Other notes	1 This is the _____ module of your course. It allows you to look at a range of different issues, happenings and events in the life of Jesus. 2 This work will complement coursework research study and presentation skills. 3 There will/will not be a test at the end of the module.

Signed _____ (student)

Signed _____ (teacher)

Attendance check   1 2 3 4 5 6 7 8 9 10

Task check   1 2 3 4 5 6 7 8 9 10 11 12 13 14

LIFE AND TEACHING OF JESUS

Teacher Module/Topic Assessment

Name of student _____

Skills	Grade	Comment
Finding out (research)		
Knowledge		
Understanding and explanation		
Judgement and evaluation		
Written (recording)		
Spoken work, including reporting back		
Graphical/creative		
Empathy (seeing from another point of view)		

Neatness

Group work and getting on with others

Effort

Presentation

Overall comment

Teacher Assessment of Targets

Task	Target	Mark	Comment
1	Account recorded		
2	Explanation, understanding of significance, meaning, symbols		
3	Empathy		
4	Oral and group work and social skills		
5	Independent work and use of other resources		

Effort

Presentation

Overall comment

Signed _____ (teacher)

Signed _____ (student)
(After discussion with your teacher, if necessary.)

Record of student's tasks

Title of task _____

1	
2	
3	
4	
5	
6	
7	
8	

Grade-related criteria (Levels of Attainment)

Skills	Level 1	Level 2	Level 3	Level 4
Research	Can say what happened.	Can find out more about it.	Can use background information to help explain and understand.	Can carry out independent study.
Empathy	Can understand people's feelings.	Can see both points of view.	Can undersand a religious and a non-religious way of looking at life.	Can enter into the tradition of others.
Understanding	Can understand basic facts of a story or event.	Understands simple cause–effect relationships and meanings of words.	Understands complicated cause–effect relationships such as chain reactions. Has the ability to transfer ideas to similar situations, e.g. relating parable to its meaning.	Can appreciate the complex nature of relationships and question the quality of evidence.
Explanation	Can give simple answers to direct questions.	Can give simple answers to show *why* this or that may be the case. Also what the effect will be.	Can produce a thoughtful and ordered account that is well put together and can give more than one possible explanation. A *basic* argument.	Can produce a thoughtful and logical essay that includes graphical material that is relevant to some explanations considered.
Judgement and evaluation	Can give a simple response to the information given.	Can reconsider simple evidence given more details.	Can re-think evidence given, where there may not be just one right answer.	Can take all evidence into account and see possible 'weaknesses' and weigh the importance—from which a 'balanced' decision based on the facts can be made.
Written	Can write simple sentences.	Can write simple sentences with simple clauses. Can write short paragraphs to show understanding of the material.	Very competent in the use of language. Is able to choose appropriate styles of expression to suit purpose(s).	Competent in basic skills and can write using fairly competent sentences. Is able to use different styles of expression (newspaper reports, letters, etc.)
Spoken	Can give answers to questions.	Can offer views on questions put to the group. Gets involved in group work and simple role-play.	Is able to present a prepared case to a large group or class.	Is capable of discussing an issue, answering other pupils' ideas and points of view, and can cope with complex role-play situations.
Graphical	Is able to read and make simple bar charts and understand simple sketch maps related to facts.	Is able to read and make more complicated graphs and charts. Has a good understanding of how to use photos, pictures and maps.	Is able to read and make different types of graphs and charts and make personal selection of methods to represent facts. Can read off charts and diagrams and also maps.	Can read and make sense of, plan, select and construct maps, graphs, charts and diagrams to meet the needs of the task.
Creative	Can add artwork to the task by colouring charts, diagrams, etc. Can make a suitable cover for work.	Can experiment with ideas and try out different forms of presenting work. Has ideas about how to tackle a task.	Is imaginative in the tasks set, such as role-play or design.	Has a good degree of originality in presenting ideas in art form. Is good at devising tasks and expressing ideas artistically.
Neatness	Work is presented according to the basic rules of presentation with only minor mistakes and things left out.	Work is always correctly presented according to the rules of presentation with-out too much help from teacher.	Is able to visualize, plan and lay out a page of work using a range of skills.	Is able to design a project using an index or contents page. Can introduce a project and draw conclusions in a clear, tidy and interesting way.
Social	Can work well with one friend.	Can work well in a well-defined activity such as an opinion poll.	Can contribute actively to a group discussion or other group task.	Can organize a group to co-operate and plan and carry out a complicated task.

Student's self-assessment

Topic _____

How I found out
What I can talk about
What I now understand
How I feel about giving my opinions and listening to others' opinions
How I feel about recording ideas
How I feel about explaining to others
What I now understand (including symbols, meaning)
What I have learnt about how this connects with our life today

How much effort I have put into the work

Grade myself _____

Student's signature _____

Teacher's comment

LIFE AND TEACHING OF JESUS